# Our
# Seattle

Text by Barbara Sleeper
Photography by Mike Sedam

Voyageur Press

*Still Raining, Still Dreaming* by Jimi Hendrix on page 89 used by permission of Rebecca Wilcots, Experience Hendrix.

Edited by Todd R. Berger
Designed by Andrea Rud
Cover designed by Maria Friedrich
Printed in China

02    03    04    05    06    6    5    4    3    2

Library of Congress Cataloging-in-Publication Data available.
ISBN 0-89658-007-5


Published by Voyageur Press, Inc.
123 North Second Street, P.O. Box 338, Stillwater, MN 55082 U.S.A.
651-430-2210, fax 651-430-2211


**Educators, fundraisers, premium and gift buyers, publicists, and marketing managers:** Looking for creative products and new sales ideas? Voyageur Press books are available at special discounts when purchased in quantities, and special editions can be created to your specifications. For details contact the marketing department at 800-888-9653.

**Page 1:** *Seattle's maritime charm is captured in this still life of a vintage boat tied up at the Wooden Boat Center on Lake Union. Surrounded on three sides by water, Seattle is a boat-lover's paradise.*

**Page 4:** *The renovated Pioneer Square historic area was once the heart of Seattle's early business district. While the opium dens, "seamstresses," and bathhouses of Seattle's fabled gold rush era are long gone, what remains are the historic buildings and tall tales, best experienced on a Seattle Underground Tour.*

**Page 5:** *This handmade sign captures the good-natured informality of life in the Pacific Northwest. You almost have to love seafood to live here, as* fruits de la mar *are featured at local restaurants and markets, sold dockside, and from roadside truck tailgates.*

# Dedication

To my parents, Norma and William H. Sleeper, with gratitude for a childhood filled with love and laughter . . . and to my wild brother, Bill Sleeper, whose legacy of humorous sibling pranks is woven with great affection through every line in this book.

—Barbara Sleeper

To my dear friends Anny, Jeannie, and Dr. Diana Fairbanks, who did everything from tote camera gear to double park while I shot images for this book. I am especially grateful to my three children, Michelle, Chad, and Quinn, who have filled my life with joy and colorful memories. And you too, Mom!

—Mike Sedam

# Acknowledgments

From fact-checking to proofreading, heartfelt appreciation goes to the many people who helped with the preparation of this book. I would like to thank the staff in the Archives and Special Collections Division of the University of Washington Library for their invaluable assistance and patience. They came up with an answer, or an additional reference, with each new question I asked. Special thanks go to friend and colleague Claudia Mirchel at the Seattle-King County Convention and Visitors Bureau for providing facts, contacts, and quotes during the research and writing of this book, and to David Blandford of the Seattle-King County News Bureau for his enthusiasm and invaluable assistance. Much appreciation goes to editor, Todd Berger, who made this project a delight from start to finish. I would also like to thank my dear Seattle friends, George Schnibbe, Helen Rodway, Tom Boyden, Marilyn Hedges, Gail Knapp Merrick, Elaine Gorud, Carol Farhrenbruch, Linda Toy, Cindy Jones, Jan Wagner, and Eric Dahl for the years of shared fun and memories that are an important part of this book. And finally, extra special thanks go to my three sweet kids, Kelly, David and Josh. You are the best!

—Barbara Sleeper

# Contents

# Introduction

"This is still a frontier city, not only geographically, but of the human spirit
as well. It is a place of new beginnings, fresh starts, and leaps of faith.
A place where people with new ideas in the arts, sciences, and
business might hear an encouraging word."
—Paul Owen Lewis, artist and author

I first fell in love with Seattle as an impressionable eight-year-old. In 1958, my father, an engineer employed by the General Electric Company, was asked to represent GE on radio guidance work for Boeing's Dyna-Soar Program, an attempt to design a re-entry glider like the later space shuttle. To entice our family to relocate from Syracuse, New York, to Seattle for the ten-month assignment, my Dad regaled our family with wild tales of snow-capped volcanoes, Indians, roaring rivers, evergreen forests, and giant slugs. The tall tales worked.

For some reason, it was the description of giant slugs that stuck in my mind during our three-thousand-mile cross-country camping adventure. Upon arriving in Seattle, I immediately rushed into the salal and sword fern woods behind our house in search of the fabled mollusks. With bare hands, I gathered up every slug that I could find and put them in a jar for observation—big ones, little ones, and several of the huge six-

**Above:** *Warm summer days draw squealing, giggling kids into the spray of the International Fountain located at the heart of the Seattle Center. The inviting, circular design of the fountain, together with its animated water and music shows, is a central gathering place for young and old alike. Because the 287 water nozzles turn on and off electronically to music, the daring fountain runners never know when they will be hit next, or from where. This makes it great fun for kids, as well as for dry adults watching from the sidelines.*

**Facing page:** *The ever-present Space Needle is reflected in the mirrored windows of the Fourth and Vine Building near the Seattle Center. Such fanciful imagery of art and architecture, combined with the city's stunning physical setting, has made Seattle one of the most beautiful cities in the country—an inspirational haven for artists and entrepreneurs alike. With a motto first coined in the 1880s, Seattle has worked hard "to become what Nature made her: the Queen City of the Northwest." Since 1981, she has been referred to simply as the "Emerald City."*

inch spotted leopard slugs. I was in slug heaven.

It was only after the thrill of the hunt was over, trophies in hand, that I discovered the insidious qualities of slug slime. The slimy secretion—left behind as sun-glistened slug trails over vegetation, across sidewalks, and up and down house walls—is almost impossible to remove from your skin. This single fact, gleaned from that first hands-on, slime-off experience with slugs back in 1958, has remained with me to this day. It marked the poignant beginning of a forty-year love affair with Seattle and the Pacific Northwest.

During our family's brief transfer to Seattle, my peripatetic Dad took us smelt fishing on the storm-swept beaches of the Pacific Ocean, searching for agates and Japanese floats along those same shores, exploring the ice caves and wild-flowered meadows of Mount Rainier, and spontaneously touring Indian reservations during exploratory drives around the remote, rain-forested, moss-draped Olympic Peninsula. He also got our family up at three in the morning to drive miles in the dark to compete in Boeing's once-annual Salmon Derby. I have particularly fond memories of those predawn fishing trips on Puget Sound, spent curled up in a fetal position for warmth at the bow of our tiny boat, catching dogfish—but never a salmon.

At the end of Dad's assignment in Seattle, our family moved back to New York. But the damage had been done. It would be the last winter I would ever zip up in a snowsuit to trudge off to school in sub-arctic temperatures. Seattle's slugs, surround-Sound mountains, evergreen forests, scenic waterways, and the lingering essence of salmon beckoned—not only to me, but to the entire family as well. Within a year we were back in the Emerald City, settled into our old neighborhood, with Dad now employed by Boeing.

Our house, like many in the Seattle suburbs, sat at the edge of a Douglas fir ravine frequented by raccoon bandits, nocturnal flying squirrels, mountain beavers, squawking Steller's jays—and slugs. A gurgling, frequently flooded creek coursed its way through the ravine on its way to nearby Puget Sound. This magical backyard proved fertile ground for endless childhood adventures and outdoor exploration. It was the ideal habitat for an animal-loving, nature-oriented tomboy.

We blazed trails, collected animal skulls, raced miniature boats down the creek, had horsetail fern fights, held neighborhood pet shows, and feasted on salmonberries, huckleberries, and plump summer blackberries. We even tried smoking the dried stems of sword ferns, and one day, high school pal Darlene Bush and I dodged freighter waves to row an eight-foot dingy right across Puget Sound.

In the spring, delicate trilliums emerged against the trademark Northwest fragrance of skunk cabbage and cherry blossoms. Beach walks along Puget Sound, rope-swing-aided jumps into streams, more dogfish derbies, and summer nights spent sleeping in the backyard under the stars, etched indelible memories across my childhood. It was a happy childhood—I don't remember that it ever rained.

When we first moved to Seattle, the Smith Tower was the tallest building in the city, and the Space Needle and Interstate 5 had yet to be built. Traffic wasn't an issue, native salmon were still abundant, and old-growth cathedral forests were peacefully growing older. Spotted owls had yet to become an endangered species, young Jimi Hendrix was busy practicing his guitar, and future *Far Side* cartoonist, Gary Larson, was a local elementary school kid who liked to hang out in swamps.

Back then, no one suspected that Seattle was destined to become the espresso capital of the world, spawn a mega-Microsoft, start a revolution in recreational clothing and equipment and become America's premier alpine climbing center, or dictate world fashion and music through "grunge." And who would have guessed that Mount St. Helens would soon blow its top off?

For decades, Seattle had been one of the country's best-kept secrets. If you had asked Easterners in the 1950s about Seattle, they'd typically shrug and mumble something about tall trees and Indians. Wasn't that the place where it rained all the time? At best Seattle was considered a remote outpost in the far northwest corner of the Lower 48, an uncultured processing center for fish and trees. Word hadn't leaked out yet of the Pacific Northwest's tranquil natural beauty—of the mild maritime climate, wrap-around mountains, and fjordlike waterways.

Also overlooked was the spiritual impact that such a physically beautiful setting could have on

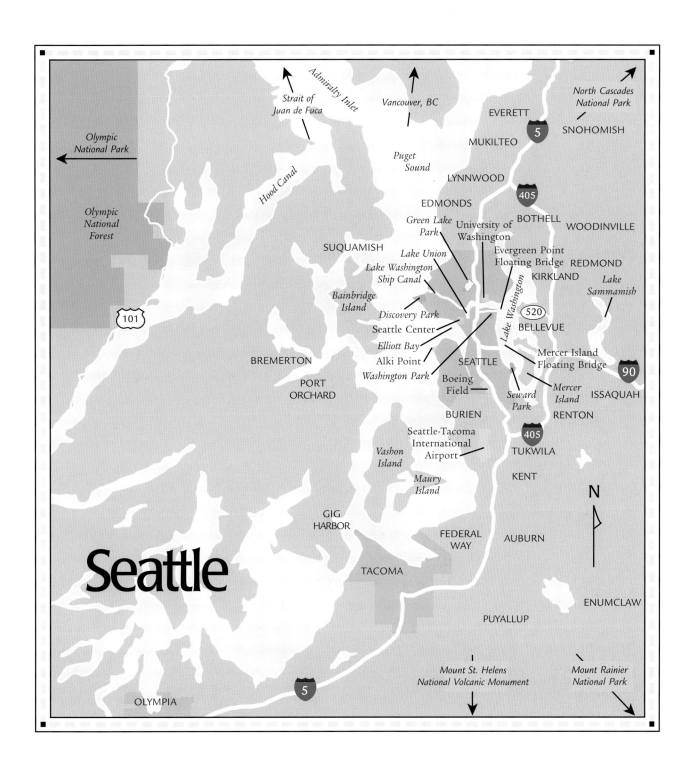

temperament and culture. This spirituality is expressed in the rich decorative art, legends, and traditions of the Northwest coastal tribes, whose totem poles, carved ceremonial masks, woven baskets, and ornately decorated button blankets hint of a sacred time past. Currently, the spirituality translates into polite, courteous drivers; generous community-based philanthropy; a proliferation of the arts; rampant entrepreneurialism; and a legacy of environmental activism.

Seattleites are indeed concerned about the quality of life and the environment. The voluntary simplicity movement—a more natural approach to life based on the pursuit of friendship, health, and personal interests rather than corporate and economic goals—is big here, and more than 90 percent of Seattleites now recycle. According to Bill Radke, morning anchor for KUOW-FM, during the 1995 American League Division Series, a Seattle Mariner hit a home run and hundreds of Yankee fans threw garbage onto the field. "Seattle fans are so nice," joked Radke, "that they went down to the field and separated the garbage into paper, aluminum, and glass for recycling."

There is definitely something about life in Seattle that twists one's sense of humor. As a kid, I grew up with slogans such as "Seattle: Twenty million slugs can't be wrong!" and "Seattleites don't tan, they just rust." *Seattle Times* columnist Emmett Watson claims the constant cloudiness and frequent drizzle turns Seattle into a sort of urban car wash from November to March, and that our muted colors resemble the underside of a mushroom.

Such irreverent Northwest humor is attributable, in part, to Seattle's colorful history. Founded by a band of free-spirited pioneers who landed at Alki Point in 1851, Seattle literally rose up from the quagmire. The five women among the members of the original landing party reportedly wept when they caught sight of their promised land—an ominous

*Seattle's dramatic skyline, photographed from Beacon Hill at sunset, is in constant flux. The city's downtown area is in the middle of a $1.4 billion building boom. In the works is a new World Trade Center, expanded retail and office space, and a South city makeover that will include a new pro-baseball stadium, a Union Station facelift, and a new pro-football stadium. A $3.9 billion Sound Transit project is also being planned.*

gray wilderness. Winter storms washed away the first settlement, so a second one, dubbed Duwamps, was founded on the tideflats of the Duwamish River.

The name Duwamps was changed to Seattle in honor of Chief Sealth, Seattle being the phonetic spelling of the chief's name. According to Roberta Frye Watt in her 1931 book *Four Wagons West*, the revered leader of the local Suquamish and Allied tribes "was not favorably impressed" by this switch because of his tribal belief that every time a dead man's name is spoken after his death, he will roll over in his grave. Chief Sealth convinced David "Doc" Maynard and other prominent business leaders that a town named in his honor would be a disturbance to his ghost. To ameliorate any posthumous inconvenience Sealth might suffer while spinning in his grave, local businessmen chipped in each year to generate what amounted to a "chief tax," which was paid to Sealth for nearly twenty years until he died.

According to author Bill Speidel in his book *Sons of the Profits*, this "tax" turned out to be a wise investment. In 1855, just four years after white settlers landed at Alki, and a year after Washington became a territory, a year of small Indian skirmishes led to a treaty that forced the Seattle-area tribes to move to a reservation at Suquamish on the Kitsap Peninsula. As the articulate leader of six Puget Sound tribes, Chief Sealth convinced his people not to participate in the Battle of Seattle, mounted by other Pacific Northwest tribes on January 26, 1856. This one-day Indian uprising, in justifiable protest over their loss of land and rights, was settled quietly, but the resulting publicity succeeded in slowing Seattle's growth for nearly a decade.

With patch-and-go city planning and a rainy season that seemed to last all year, fledgling Seattle was easier to navigate by rowboat than on foot. In fact, it was possible to row southeast from Pioneer Square to Seventh Avenue. High tide invariably left shops flooded and feet wet. Even the residents of Seattle's first graveyard near Fifth Avenue and Jackson Street were afloat during high tide. Houses, streets, and train tracks, even the first primitive water system, were elevated on wooden stilts to escape the mud.

The term "skid road," meaning an unsavory part of town, originated in Seattle's historic Pioneer Square area. This is where loggers built the original Skid Road from the top of Yesler Way down to Henry Yesler's steam-powered sawmill on the waterfront—the first on Puget Sound. Logs were rolled down over saplings greased with dogfish oil. Brothels and saloons thrived south of this Yesler Way "sin line." North of it lay the respectable part of town. Appropriate for Seattle's soggy tideflats and timber beginning, supplying dock pilings to San Francisco, the early settlers were nicknamed "mossbacks."

The need for pioneering pluck and humor continued when flushing toilets arrived. The toilets worked just fine; it was the overtaxed sewer system running down Seattle's steep hillsides that didn't. Twice a day, Seattle's sea-level toilets geysered with high tide. This made it necessary to consult the daily tide tables before taking a trip to the john. The *Seattle Post-Intelligencer* obliged by printing the tide tables on the front page. In an effort to outdistance the high-tide eruptions, a few ingenious folks elevated their toilets on platforms ten feet in the air.

With sidewalks built substantially higher than the streets, fun-loving dandies took advantage of the elevation to spit tobacco juice on passengers in carriages. Such a chaotic environment also spawned the self-proclaimed "pluguglies," a group of rowdy young men who dressed up as jesters on the Fourth of July, painted their faces black, and tore up the streets of Pioneer Square in a horse-drawn lumber wagon.

Seattle's first roads were so bad that newspaper editorials warned that every wagon should come equipped with a life raft—in the event it should sink out of sight in the mud. When ten-year-old Joseph Bufonchio drowned in a giant chuckhole at Third Avenue South and Jackson Street, a local reporter described the event as if drownings in Seattle's city streets were commonplace. He irreverently described a "delighted" crowd of two thousand who gathered to watch "several other laughable incidents" that followed, as first the boy's distraught father fell into the mudhole, followed by a boxer named Chicago Ed.

Incorporated as a town in 1865, disincorporated in 1867, and reincorporated in 1869, Seattle had a fitful start. At one time the populace consisted of more rats than people. According to Roger Sale in *Seattle Past and Present*, the original settlers were independent people who attracted independent

*Anyone who moves to the Pacific Northwest must make their own peace with slugs—as these slimy herbivores are everywhere. The shell-less, night-grazing mollusks munch seedlings, strip marigolds bare, and generally leave slime trails in the most unlikely places.*

people to join them in their fight to start a new city. Such individuality ultimately lead to diversity of local commerce and manufacturing, and, in turn, economic independence.

But according to Clarence Bagley in his 1916 *History of Seattle*, their biggest fight was not against the elements, but against the Northern Pacific Railroad, which did not recognize the existence of Seattle and did everything in its power to force her citizens to abandon their homes and move to Tacoma, where the railroad owned the land and hoped to build the one great city on Puget Sound.

When the Northern Pacific received a charter in 1864 to build a line from Lake Superior to some point on Puget Sound, excitement in the Northwest reached a fever pitch. Every settlement on the Sound had hopes of being chosen as the transcontinental terminus. Seattle seemed the natural choice as it had the largest population, and coal deposits had just been discovered in King County. Realizing the economic importance of such a rail connection, Seattle offered the railroad seventy-five hundred town lots, three thousand acres of land, $200,000 in bonds, $50,000 in cash, and the use of a considerable portion of its waterfront for a depot and terminal tracks.

A year later, on July 14, 1873, the railroad commission announced the terminus would be located on Tacoma's Commencement Bay. Tacoma had won the transcontinental bid, and in the sixteen ensuing years, the Northern Pacific monopoly did everything it could to squeeze the economic life out of Seattle.

A more devastating blow to Seattle's enthusiastic populace could hardly be imagined. A few folks did pull up stakes and move to Tacoma, but those that remained were undaunted in their quest for a railroad. Lacking the needed capital, residents decided to do the work themselves. On May 1, 1874, the entire population of Seattle gathered at Steele's Landing on the Duwamish River to build their own railroad. The men and boys worked all day on grading, while the women prepared food. It was agreed that each man would give one day a week of voluntary labor until the road topped Snoqualmie Pass and dropped down the other side. News of Seattle's pluck and determination quickly reached the outside world and enticed eager young men from the East to emigrate to Seattle to join in the fight.

Seattle's single-minded quest for a railroad connection is a remarkable story of hard work and political intrigue. By 1875, five miles of railroad were completed from Steele's Landing on the Duwamish to the coal mines of Renton. An extension to the mines of Newcastle followed. Meanwhile, the first Great Northern train from the East reached Puget Sound during the summer of 1893. However, it would take another sixteen years before the last rail was laid over Snoqualmie Pass in 1909. In 1910, the Oregon-Washington Railroad ran its first train into Seattle, and a year later, Seattle's magnificent Union Pacific Terminal was completed.

"Seattle fought her (railroad) battle single-handed through stress and storm, until she emerged the victor. There is absolutely no other city in America with such a record," wrote Bagley. "Nothing cements a people like a menace of danger from the outside; this was the underlying force that spurred every Seattle citizen on to deeds of civic valor in the early days." In the end, Seattle could almost be grateful to the Northern Pacific for providing such an impetus, because on May 1, 1874, when residents pitched in with picks and shovels to build their own railroad, the infamous "Seattle Spirit" was born.

The ultimate test of the Seattle Spirit, however, was yet to come. On June 6, 1889, a pot of burning glue in a cabinetmaker's shop ignited the Great Seattle Fire. Instant urban renewal was accomplished in less than a day, when thirty city blocks were incinerated—along with a million rats. Four days later, even after their office and presses were destroyed, the *Seattle Times* managed to publish an edition and proclaim: "SEATTLE DISFIGURED, but still in the ring, this is the song Seattle will sing, New buildings, New hope, New streets, New town, there's nothing that can throw Seattle down. . . ."

Three weeks later, the city passed an ordinance to raise the existing city streets between eight to thirty-five feet within a forty-four-block area near the Waterfront. Taking several years to complete, the project put an end to geysering toilets and permanently entombed Seattle's original sidewalks and ground-floor shops underground. As the first turn-of-the-century "subterranean mall," the underground shops remained open until 1907, when they were finally declared a fire trap and abandoned.

Like a phoenix rising from the ashes, Seattle benefited from the $10 million disaster. Within two years of the fire, Seattle's business quarter was considered finer, more convenient, and more modern than that of any other city of similar size. During Seattle's transformation from a mud-and-wood-plank frontier town to a carefully designed city of stone and brick, an estimated thirty-five hundred buildings were constructed—most within the burned area.

In 1880, there were 3,553 residents. By 1885, 12,000 people lived in Seattle, most within ten blocks of Yesler Way. However, people had begun to take notice of this fledgling town, and by 1890, the population grew to 42,837. With the opportunity for investment after the Great Fire, the arrival of the first Great Northern transcontinental train to Puget Sound in 1893, and the discovery of Klondike gold in 1897, a population explosion ensued as settlers moved west. By 1900, 80,671 people called Seattle home. Just ten years later, that number nearly tripled to 237,174.

At the start of the gold rush in 1897, a census revealed that a remarkable 10 percent of these tax-paying souls were employed as "seamstresses" in Pioneer Square's notorious "Tenderloin District." For three years the busy seamstresses generated enough revenue in licensing fees to fund 87 percent of the city's annual budget—vice and prostitution "outstripped" Seattle's timber industry at the turn of the century.

Because Seattle was founded on a small spit of land surrounded by mudflats and cliffs, the industrious residents were forced to mold the natural elements in order to build their city. Over a fifty-five-year period beginning in 1876, they scraped, sluiced, and shifted more than fifty million tons of earth all over town. An estimated sixty different regrade projects were initiated to level and recontour Seattle's hilly profile, at times turning the city into a lunar landscape. First Avenue was flattened between Yesler and Pike, all 4,354,625 cubic yards of Denny Hill were recycled, and more than two thousand acres of tidelands were reclaimed in the harbor. Even so, six major hills still remain, including First Hill which early residents called "Profanity Hill" because it was such a "bleeping expletive" to climb.

As the young city took form, Seattle began to make a name for itself. In 1909, the elaborate Alaska-Yukon-Pacific Exposition opened on the University of Washington campus to celebrate Seattle's decade-long success in outfitting and exploiting gold-rush Alaska and the Yukon. It was hoped that Asia would be next. According to Paul Dorpat in his 1984 book *Seattle Now and Then,* the 108-day event "opened on time and paid for itself," attracting nearly four million visitors. The main attraction was the Arctic Circle, a dazzling white semicircle of seven neoclassical and baroque buildings surrounding the Cascades waterfall and Geyser Basin, a circular artificial pool now called Frosh Pond at the University of Washington campus. The sideshow of "primitive and exotic carny attractions" called the Pay Streak drew the biggest crowds. Among the acts featured were the loinclothed Igorrotes from the Philippines, Q & A with Albert the Educated Horse, and Princess Azmara's love dance with snakes.

Then along came legendary restaurateur Ivar Haglund, a name long synonymous with excellent Seattle seafood. For more than sixty years, Ivar honored mollusks in "keep clam" songs, recipes, and puns. The bivalves helped Haglund clam his way to fame and fortune with witty ballads like "Run, Clam, Run." The mollusk mogul, who died in 1985, was perpetually in the Seattle limelight. To help publicize a small aquarium he opened on Pier 54 in 1936, he wheeled a seal named Patsy in a baby carriage to see Santa Claus at the Bon Marche department store. To draw attention to his newly opened Ivar's Acres of Clams restaurant, he held a series of public clam-eating contests; one contestant wolfed down 337 clams in ten minutes. According to Haglund, it wasn't a pretty sight. However, Ivar's famous chowders and deep-fried fish and shellfish have kept customers happy since he opened his first seafood bar in 1938.

"Clam nectar is a rejuvenator," claimed Ivar. "A shot of whiskey just doesn't have the same appeal as a shot of clam nectar."

In the sixties, Seattle humorist Bill Speidel began poking around the dusty archives in the Seattle Public Library and visiting the long-forgotten haunts of old Skid Road. He discovered the "city beneath a city" buried below Pioneer Square—Seattle's own version of the ruins of Pompeii—and, while admittedly drunk, got the idea for an underground tour. Dubbed the Father of the Seattle Underground, Speidel offered his first tour into the city's historic bowels on Know Your Seattle Day, May 31, 1965. More than five hundred people lined up for the event. Speidel's humorous tours and ensuing books helped mobilize the city to designate eighteen square blocks of Pioneer Square a national historic site in 1970.

Although Bill Speidel died in 1988, his irreverent Underground Tours are still offered daily. They begin in Doc Maynard's Public House, an authentically restored 1890s saloon located in Pioneer Square. Participants are typically thanked for joining the only truly tacky tour remaining in the United States and are then told that the no-refund policy is now in effect. The guide assures everyone that there will be no free rides for kids, no spooky plastic people, and no pop-up hippos waiting down below. However, the tour will be entering an area condemned in 1907 as a fire trap, a subterranean world filled with antique air, loose bricks, creaky steps, dripping pipes, spiderwebs the envy of Hollywood—and rats. This offbeat tour remains one of Seattle's most popular attractions.

Even when Boeing hit the skids in the late 1960s, laying off 64,000 of its 101,000 employees, humor prevailed. Someone paid for a billboard that read, "Will the last person leaving Seattle please turn out the lights?"

It was about this time that Bigfoot sightings increased, maybe because so many unemployed people had time on their hands. This elusive, hairy creature of Northwest legend has never been captured, but Sasquatch has certainly left its humongous footprints across our regional psyche—spawning namesake festivals, bagels, donuts, taverns, and big-foot chocolates. There's even an international Sasquatch Symposium each year, "a gathering of believers and skeptics devoted to the Northwest's most famous mystery beast."

Funny things just seem to happen in Seattle. A few years ago, the Bon Marche department store attached a huge, inflated King Kong to the side of its downtown building, only to have it blown down the street in a windstorm. At times, the Space Needle is decorated to look like a UFO, the effect enhanced when its base is concealed in a thick blanket of fog. During the construction of the towering Columbia Seafirst Center, the tallest building in Seattle, an enormous American flag was draped down one side, with signs posted to keep residents advised of progress toward the top. When the scaffolding finally reached the seventy-sixth floor, a party was thrown—and another King Kong inflated.

Last year Interstate 5 was closed by a giant tossed salad—after a produce truck crashed. The freeway was closed again near Mount Vernon when a man danced buck naked for three hours on the top of a freight truck—just out of reach of state troopers. Underscoring Seattle's addiction to coffee, a female inmate escaped from a King County jail in 1997, only to be busted three blocks away when she stopped for a latte. Former Mayor Norm Rice holds the distinction of winning the Funniest Mayor Competition—possibly due to a voice trick that enables

him to sound as if he's talking underwater. None of this seems out of character when you realize that Washington State voters almost succeeded in making "Louie, Louie" by the Kingsmen the official state song.

Possibly Seattleites look to the lighter side because we are now overdue for a major earthquake, and it turns out nearby Mount Rainier isn't so dormant afterall. Maybe it's the fact that since 1997, mudslides have increasingly closed roads and pushed waterfront houses into Puget Sound, and more frequent winter avalanches in the Cascades can be downright inconvenient, if not deadly.

The weather definitely plays an important part in shaping our regional humor and schizophrenic temperament. One minute it can be sunny, the next it can be hailing, covering the ground in instant, icy white, followed by a brilliant double rainbow. Meteorologists report the passing of "rain cells" over specific parts of the city—and describe "rooster tails" in reference to the driving conditions during black cloud deluges. It is possible to die by hydroplaning

on our freeways—but then again, the rainbows are spectacular.

Many of us missed Bill Clinton's first inaugural day speech on January 20, 1993, due to a windstorm that knocked down trees, telephone poles, and power lines. A similar storm left thousands of families with half-cooked turkeys on Thanksgiving Day in 1983. Possibly the reason Seattleites are so friendly is that natural disasters tend to be bonding experiences. They get folks talking to each other out on the streets, in grocery lines, and while waiting in emergency rooms—especially when there is no electricity. And there's nothing like a small earthquake to light up the phone lines. Winter flood warnings for rivers in western Washington routinely get people out sandbagging together.

The first few pages in the Seattle Metro Telephone Directory are the most revealing about life in the Northwest. They include detailed emergency preparedness information for floods, earthquakes, severe thunderstorms—and tsunamis, or tidal waves. Hundreds of blue-and-white Tsunami Hazard Zone

*Wrapped in early morning mist, Reflection Lake in Mount Rainier National Park takes on an almost ethereal quality. It is a scene that captures the natural beauty of alpine lakes and evergreen forests typical of the Pacific Northwest.*

signs are now being posted up and down the Washington State coastline, warning folks to run for high ground when they feel the ground shake.

Naturally, conditions like these play hell with our roads, which leads to another favorite humor category—potholes. Potholes are a long-standing tradition in Seattle. Following the rough winter of 1997, the city averaged more than 245 pothole complaints a month. Callers were asked to carefully describe the size and exact location of each pothole. Based on the speed with which they have been repaired, the pothole data was apparently collected and deep-sixed in a time capsule to be opened next century. Seattle now ranks ninth on the national Pothole Index.

As a city surrounded on three sides by water, Seattle devised ways to span these roads—however potholed—over bodies of water large and small. As with everything else, Seattleites got inventive. "Se-

attle is the only place in the world that has *floating* bridges," quips nightclub comedian Chris Alpine. "The rest of the world has steel and concrete bridges." In fact, two floating bridges span the width of Lake Washington to connect downtown Seattle with the eastside cities of Bellevue, Mercer Island, Kirkland, and Redmond.

Wild windstorms may occasionally slow traffic on a wave-washed floating bridge, but Seattle's numerous drawbridges take the crab cake when it comes to disrupting traffic. Seattle is the self-proclaimed pleasure boat capital of the world, and boats, not cars, have the right of way in the Emerald City. At the first sign of a tall mast, down go the traffic gates and up pops a drawbridge. Sometimes the bridges get stuck—but never, it seems, in the down position.

The official opening of the Seattle boating season is on the first Saturday in May. It is a busy time for drawbridges. Festively decorated yachts parade from the Ballard locks through Lake Union to Lake Washington, tripping drawbridges as they go. The Opening Day Boat Parade, sponsored by the Seattle Yacht Club, includes just about anything that can float.

But boats aren't the only thing on the move in this city—Seattleites are blatantly athletic. Should someone ask you what you do, they aren't referring to your occupation. Natives jog, bike, skate, and walk all over town. Windsurfers don wet suits to ride gale waves across Lake Union. Others water-ski and Jet Ski around Lake Washington, even in winter. Cars toting snow skis, snowboards, snowshoes, canoes, or kayaks are a common sight around Seattle, as are hot-air balloons rising over Woodinville. University of Washington English professor and Seattle historian Roger Sale once claimed that "Seattle has no day too cold, and few too hot, for hard work and exercise. . . . it offers no excuses not to be one's best." With such a fanatic outdoor focus and given Seattle's often rainy skies, it is little wonder that native dress consists mostly of parkas and raincoats, though rarely an umbrella. Here, men stroll the streets of Ballard in hipwaders and women wear jeans to the opera.

Walk down any street in Seattle and another thing becomes immediately apparent. Seattle is an ethnic and cultural melting pot. Just about every religion, nationality, and shade of skin can be found in this racially hip, harmonious city. The many ethnic festivals, restaurants, and cultural celebrations give Seattle an international flair that makes it possible to experience the world without even leaving the city. Native American, Asian, Scandinavian, Italian, Hispanic, and African-American influences are particularly strong here, and interracial marriages are common. In 1990, Norm Rice became Seattle's first African-American mayor, and in 1996, Washington's Gary Locke was elected America's first Chinese-American governor.

In 1903, James R. Meikle identified the Seattle Spirit as "the spirit that takes hold of everyone who becomes a resident of this city and inspires him with energy, enterprise, and enthusiasm." Based on the proliferation of art, industry, and high-tech invention occurring in the Northwest, such words ring true. Seattle is a city of firsts: Northgate Mall, the world's first covered shopping center, opened here in 1950. Seattle resident Elizabeth Julesberg (alias Elizabeth Montgomery) penned the Dick and Jane children's books here. And Robert Joffrey launched his famous ballet company in Seattle. The game Pictionary, the yellow "Happy Face" logo, dog toothbrushes, and The Wave all evolved here.

As a mecca for artists and entrepreneurs, Seattle is the birthplace of a remarkable number of enterprises, including: United Parcel Service (UPS); Paccar; Nordstroms; REI; Eddie Bauer; the Bon Marche; Jay Jacobs; Starbucks Coffee Company; Costco; and AT&T Wireless Services (McCaw Cellular Communications). In 1996, Boeing acquired aerospace and weapons leader Rockwell International, and in 1997, Boeing and McDonnell Douglas merged to form the largest aerospace company in the world. As the world leader in commercial airplanes, military aircraft, and space exploration, the new Boeing now employs more than 220,000 people. This book-loving city is also home to "Earth's Biggest Bookstore," Amazon.com, with 2.5 million titles now posted in cyberspace. And since 1976, just about everyone has benefited from the creative genius of Bill Gates and Paul Allen when they started the computer software revolution with Microsoft. Fifteen hundred computer hardware and software development firms are now located in the Seattle area.

This high-energy, high-profile, high-tech proliferation of start-up businesses has contributed to Seattle's booming economy—and joie de vivre lifestyle. Here natives can be seen driving convertibles with the top down during light summer showers, daredevils skydive off the Space Needle, and pampered, bandana-wearing boat dogs cruise the San Juan Islands on expensive yachts. It's not unusual to pass an amphibian car on the freeway, watch a motorcycle club do group wheelies as they exit a ferry, or spot outdoor crazies standing on the beach at Alki in the full wave-crashing frenzy of a winter storm. Each December over one hundred volunteers light four thousand luminaria and place them around the three-mile periphery of Green Lake, creating just one of hundreds of romantic places around town where lovers regularly enact their own version of *Sleepless in Seattle*. Not surprisingly, many romance novelists call Seattle home.

The best expression of this contagious Seattle Spirit is often overheard in public as total strangers give spontaneous testimonials about life in Seattle—

the beautiful scenery, amazing weather, or a special day-hike in the mountains. Recently, when a fifty-something woman in front of me at the store checkout was asked if she needed help with her groceries, she replied, "Thanks, I can do it myself. I've got to figure out how to load them on my motorcycle anyway."

"During the first year we lived here after moving from the East Coast," said another woman in an athletic club locker room, "I didn't understand when they announced on the radio that the 'Daughters of the Klondike' meeting had been canceled. Now, after several years of living here, I do." She was, of course, referring to Seattle's gold rush ties to the Yukon and still-apparent outdoor, athletic, frontier town mentality.

Seattleites are a wily bunch. According to national statistics, they buy more sunglasses and plastic pails, own more boats, see more movies, eat more ice cream, and read more books per capita than folks anywhere else in America. The Seattle Public Library loans out more books per capita than any other city library system in the states, possibly because 37.9 percent of Seattle's adult population has at least a four-year degree. Seattle also has the highest percentage of people biking to work compared to other American cities—an estimated four thousand to eight thousand each day, depending on the weather. It's even hard to drop dead of a heart attack in Seattle, because an estimated one out of three people you pass on the street would know how to perform CPR—if a Medic 1 vehicle didn't get to you first. Seattle's nationally acclaimed Medic 1 program was the first emergency response care system in the United States and remains one of the fastest, with an average three-to-four-minute response time.

In the end, I love Seattle because of the glad-to-be-alive sunrises and primordial sunsets over jagged mountain peaks. I love the magic, ever-changing interplay of light and rainbows over fantastic cloud formations swept in lapsed-time across the city skyline. I love the feral smell of salt air along the Waterfront, and the thick pockets of fog that roll down the trough of Puget Sound pierced by haunting foghorns, seagull cries, and the "long, short, short" blasts of ferry horns.

I love the fact that flowers bloom all year, annuals overwinter, and leaves still cling to deciduous trees in December. I love the way Seattle's romantic city lights twinkle at night, everywhere reflected softly in water. Most of all, I love the fact that a coyote can find its way into a downtown building, peregrine falcons nest on a Seattle skyscraper, black bears still roam Bellevue, and hikers need to be alert to the prescence of cougars. My heart will forever leap at the unexpected glimpse of a bald eagle soaring over the city. The possibilities are infinitely wild.

"Seattle is an enigma. It always has been," says Steve Sheppard, an Emerald City native. "No one has ever defined what Seattle is. All you know is that you're happy here, and you don't want to leave."

*The Seattle Waterfront bustles with people—and seagulls. Ivar Haglund's original Fish Bar opened on Pier 54 in 1938, followed eight years later by Ivar's Acres of Clams restaurant. Both remain popular culinary landmarks. A long-standing Seattle tradition is to get fish and chips at Ivar's Fish Bar and eat them—rain or shine—sitting under the outdoor heaters. It's a great way to enjoy the Seattle Waterfront, with fresh-air views of ferryboats and fireboats while feeding the seagulls.*

# The Spirit of Seattle: Downtown and Beyond

"No matter where my airline career takes me, Seattle is always home. Every once in a while, at the end of a long trip, dog-tired, yet knowing I still have the tough commute home ahead of me, I wonder if it is worth it. But on every flight home, the magic happens again: I see Rainier floating above the clouds, I catch a glimpse of a rainswept city bathed in "oyster light," or I see a gorgeous blue-sky day when both mountain ranges and Puget Sound are dazzling. And then I know it *is* worth it."
—Lynne Evans-Sleeper, B-767 Captain, United Airlines

**Above:** *A fish vendor with the City Fish Company shows off a large king salmon for sale at the Pike Place Market. Such giants among salmon can grow to fifty-eight inches and weigh over 120 pounds. Neatly arranged rows of fish, crabs, and enormous Alaska king crab legs, as well as piles of clams and oysters, entice all who walk by. The abundant fresh seafood and produce available here has influenced Pacific Northwest cooking. The finest Seattle restaurants work with these fresh ingredients to produce a distinctive regional cuisine.*

**Facing page:** *In 1927, prominent Seattleite Albert Sperry Kerry Sr. and his wife donated land to the City of Seattle "so that all who stop here may enjoy this view." Today, Kerry Park, located on Queen Anne Hill, provides one of the most photographed views of downtown Seattle, bathed here in the purple hues of a summer sunset. Built on a series of hills, Seattle covers eighty four-square-miles. Clever pedestrians often use the elevators in downtown buildings to ease the steep ascent from the Waterfront, exiting at street-level entrances several floors up. In 1996, an estimated 3,056,800 people lived in the greater Seattle area, encompassing King, Snohomish, Pierce, and Kitsap Counties.*

**Above left:** *Seattle's intriguing mix of new and old buildings is an architectural delight. While some of the oldest buildings are more than one hundred years old, most of the newer skyscrapers are little more than ten. For example, the tall black building pictured here is the seventy-six-story Columbia Seafirst Center, the tallest building in Seattle. Completed in 1985, the 954-foot tower is nearly twice as tall as the Space Needle, and has 1.5 million pounds of Carnelian granite in its walls and flooring. The building is famous for its unique ladies restroom on the seventy-fifth floor with a glass wall view of the city below. In 1995, medical student, Jeff Summers, sneaked to the top of the Columbia Seafirst Center and jumped off with a parachute. He slammed into the building twice before landing on the roof of a nearby bank—with a fractured skull. The steps in the foreground belong to the Henry M. Jackson Federal Building. It was here in December 1997 that a young coyote ran across the lobby and ended up trapped in an elevator until animal control could rescue him.*

**Above right:** *Completed in 1989, the fifty-six-story Two Union Square Building has won several awards for engineering excellence and design. The flag-flying, high-rise commercial office tower features a glass penthouse sloped like a wave toward the harbor, and innovative earthquake- and wind-resistant materials placed within its core interior walls. Conveniently located at freeway's edge in the heart of downtown Seattle, this sleek, modern skyscraper rises above a three-floor retail area loaded with specialty shops and restaurants. The third floor features an indoor garden complete with plants, walking paths, and a large waterfall that cascades over granite boulders.*

**Facing page:** *The forty-story 1000 Second Avenue Building turns lavender at sunset, highlighting a mosaic of office windows. It was originally called the Key Tower Building when completed in 1986, but gained its less distinctive name when the new sixty-three-story Key Tower Building was completed on Fifth Avenue in 1990. These changes underscore the speed with which Seattle is growing and changing. Downtown is growing upward, and the metropolitan area is spreading outward. The Sound Transit has laid out an action plan to develop eighty-one miles of commuter rail service from Everett, north of Seattle, to Lakewood, just south of Tacoma. Transportation improvements are needed as a million more people are expected to live in the greater Seattle area by 2020.*

Rising 605 feet above the seventy-four-acre Seattle Center, the Space Needle is a favorite place to celebrate special occasions, especially New Year's Eve, when at the stroke of midnight, the air around the Needle literally explodes with fireworks. The revolving restaurant at the top offers diners a 360-degree view of the city, mountains, and Puget Sound. An outdoor observation deck, gift shops, and bar are located above the restaurant. In 1997, the Space Needle celebrated its thirty-fifth birthday.

A father gives his young son a boost into a boy-festooned tree at the Northwest Folklife Festival. This free event is held every Memorial Day weekend at the Seattle Center, and it is one of the largest folklife festivals in the country. The well-attended celebration features more than six thousand performers and artists from one hundred different countries. The gala festival celebrates Seattle's diverse ethnic mix, as well as that of the world. A rich cultural smorgasbord of food, music, dance, and visual art is presented during the four-day event.

The neo-Gothic arches of the Pacific Science Center are another architectural landmark unique to Seattle. Positioned at the base of the Space Needle, they are visible from all over the city. The futuristic arches were designed to capture the "Century 21" theme of the 1962 World's Fair. Today, they showcase the Pacific Science Center, visited by more than one million people each year. The Center is home to robotic dinosaurs, virtual reality displays, a giant IMAX Theater, special touring exhibits, and a Spacearium that features laser shows synchronized with classical or rock music.

Built as part of the 1962 World's Fair, Seattle's famous Monorail travels on a single (mono) rail elevated twenty-five feet above the ground, from Seattle Center to the downtown retail district. After traveling a total distance of 1.2 miles, it stops at the fourth-floor station at Westlake Center. Billed as the "Train to Nowhere," Seattle's monorail holds the dubious distinction of being the only monorail in the world that travels between two buildings with food courts—all in just ninety seconds. In 1997, Seattle residents voted to develop an expanded, forty-mile monorail system within the city. A feasibility study is now underway.

"When I drive westbound on Denny Way and see the Space Needle, Elliott Bay and the Olympic Mountains, or when I'm eastbound on the Evergreen Bridge and see Lake Washington with Mt. Rainier towering above it, I know unquestionably why I still reside in Seattle."
—George L. Schnibbe Jr., Contractor, Home Sweet Home, Inc.

**Left, top:** *A couple strolls hand-in-hand along Seattle's Waterfront Park located at Pier 55. This harborside park features a large bubbling bronze fountain, a pavilion reminiscent of Stonehenge, and ample places to sit and enjoy the harbor scene. With sparkling waterfront views, orange day-glow sunsets, and silhouetted mountain peaks as a backdrop to cozy clubs, pubs, and restaurants, Seattle is definitely a city for romantics. Lovers holding hands, grabbing a spontaneous hug, or embracing for a passionate sidewalk kiss express the contagious joie de vivre spirit of Seattle. The fifty-five-story Washington Mutual Tower looms in the background. The New York Times declared the building one of the three best office buildings in the nation when it was completed in 1988. For the past five years, a pair of peregrine falcons, nicknamed Belle and Stewart, have nested on the side of the skyscraper, producing three fledglings in the spring of 1997.*

**Left, bottom:** *A family prepares to board Seattle's Waterfront Trolley, which runs from Pier 70 south along the Waterfront via Pioneer Square and the Kingdome to the International District and back. Imported from Australia, the green trolleys clank past the new Bell Harbor International Convention Center, Marina, and Odyssey Maritime Museum. They also pass the new World Trade Center, the Seattle Aquarium and neighboring Omnidome IMAX Theater, endless shops and seafood restaurants, and the infamous Ye Old Curiosity Shoppe whose collection of the weird and bizarre includes "Sylvester" the mummy in a glass case, fleas in dresses, shrunken heads, Skinny Stubbs's skeleton, Siamese-twin calves, and the Lord's Prayer printed on a grain of rice and engraved on the head of a pin. Such a wealth of activities makes Seattle fun for tourists and residents alike—especially families with children.*

**Facing page:** *Softened by fog, the pastel Seattle skyline is reflected in the calm waters of Elliott Bay. Dramatic views of the Seattle Harbor can be enjoyed from several points around the bay, including Alki Beach, where this photo was taken. Two of the best restaurants with stunning views of the Waterfront skyline are Salty's at Alki and Palisades at the Elliott Bay Marina.*

Pike Place Market is considered by many to be the soul of Seattle. Established in 1907, it is one of the oldest continuously operating farmers' markets in the United States. By 1927 more than four hundred farmers regularly gathered here to sell their produce directly to consumers. That tradition persists to this day, thanks to the grassroots efforts of Seattle architect Victor Steinbrueck, who helped mobilize the "Keep the Market" campaign in the sixties. In 1971 a public vote permanently established the site as an historic district. Today the nine-acre Market encompasses 300 permanent businesses, 100 farmers, over 150 artists and craftspeople, and more than 100 street performers who entertain at the market during the year. Come sip an espresso at the original Starbucks coffee store located here, or try one of one hundred seafood dishes served at the Athenian Inn where Sleepless in Seattle was filmed.

This much-loved, sat-upon, and frequently photographed smiling pig, dubbed Rachel, is a popular fixture at Seattle's Pike Place Market. Made possible by a gift from Fratelli's Ice Cream, the life-sized bronze piggy bank "makes wishes come true." Rachel is emptied daily, and the change goes to the Market Foundation to help support the Pike Street Market Clinic, Senior Center, Child Care Center, and Downtown Food Bank.

Playful, shell-cracking sea otters entertain visitors at the Seattle Aquarium, located along the Seattle Waterfront on Pier 59. The Aquarium features marine life native to the Pacific Northwest—including northern fur seals and "aquabatic" harbor seals—and an Underwater Dome that surrounds you with creatures from Puget Sound. The Seattle Aquarium was the first in the world to connect directly to life in the ocean: Salmon fry swim overhead in glass-paneled ceilings before release into Puget Sound, and, once mature, they return via the working Salmon Ladder that wraps around the outside of the building. A hands-on Tidepool Exhibit is also popular with kids, as is the mesmerizing, walk-through Pacific Coral Reef Exhibit. "Sea Otters at the Seattle Aquarium, 'cause they can't come to see you!"

29

Right: *The festive Seattle harbor is always bustling with ferries, freighters, tugs, and tour boats. Here, the* Veendam, *a cruise ship from the Holland America Line/West Tours, is just leaving dry dock at the Seattle shipyards on Elliott Bay. Holland America Line/West Tours now owns Gray Line Tours, which was started in Seattle in 1909. It is possible to cruise to Victoria, British Columbia, at speeds up to fifty-three miles per hour on the gas turbine Victoria Clipper IV catamaran, the fastest passenger vessel in the western hemisphere. Lunch or dinner harbor cruises can be enjoyed on the* Spirit of Puget Sound, *and Argosy Cruises offers narrated tours around the Seattle harbor, area lakes, and the Ballard locks.*

Facing page: *Two Washington State Ferries tie up at Colman Dock on Pier 52 in downtown Seattle, as Argosy tour boats and private pleasure boats crisscross the waters of Elliott Bay. Connecting cities, towns, and islands across Puget Sound and the San Juans, the Washington State Ferry system is the largest ferry system in the United States with 484 sailings every day, or 3,325 trips per week. Here the* Sealth, *named after Chief Sealth, is getting ready to head for Bremerton. It can hold 100 cars and 1,200 passengers. The jumbo ferry,* Spokane, *(named after a Native American tribe in eastern Washington) commutes to Bainbridge Island carrying up to 206 cars and 2,000 passengers. In 1997, the* Tacoma, *the biggest supercarrier in the state ferry system, began service. Weighing 5,398 tons, it can carry 212 cars and 2,500 passengers.*

"Seattle is a boater's paradise."
—George Lewis, entrepreneur

*Tourists hug the rails to watch as boats of every type and size raft up together in the Hiram M. Chittenden Locks in Ballard. It is one of the best free shows in town. Floating at sea level in salt water from Puget Sound, the boats will be raised six to twenty-six feet in fifteen minutes, depending on tides and lake levels, to meet the fresh water coming from Lake Union and Lake Washington. Each year, roughly seventy-five thousand boats pass through the Ballard locks, most without mishap. However, novice or inebriated boaters can find the experience challenging, if not dangerous. In November 1997, a tugboat smashed against a wall and sank in the large lock, closing it for nine hours.*

*In 1988, the Port of Seattle completed a $13 million redevelopment of Fishermen's Terminal to better serve the United States' North Pacific fishing fleet. The facility provides moorage for more than seven hundred vessels and a pier for resupplying and repairing large factory trawlers. It's not uncommon to see enormous fishing nets stretched out on the piers for repair. Tucked away on the south side of Ballard, the dynamic terminal supports Washington's $1.5-billion-a-year commercial fishing industry.*

**Left, top:** *The Port of Seattle, one of the largest container ports in the United States, is a major international load center with a natural deepwater harbor and post-Panamax cranes (long-reach cranes that service vessels too large to pass through the Panama Canal), providing easy access and support to the newest megaships. It encompasses more than 450 acres of container-handling space and other diverse facilities. The Port also owns and operates Sea-Tac International Airport; Fishermen's Terminal; Shilshole Bay Marina, a full-service pleasure-boating marina and sail-racing hub of Puget Sound; and 1.5 million square feet of warehouse space. Built by the Port of Seattle, the new World Trade Center, opened in 1998, will strengthen Seattle's role as a center for international trade by bringing trade-related businesses, organizations, and services under one roof.*

**Left, center:** *Tugboats on either side of the oil tanker* Allapooya Ketchikan *help maneuver the huge ship up the mouth of the Duwamish Waterway. To handle the heavy freighter traffic in and out of the harbor, the Port of Seattle works with more than thirty tug and barge operators. Transportation services are provided by an equal number of steamship operators. The Port of Seattle manages a deepwater grain terminal, a customs examination station, and a foreign trade zone that includes fourteen hundred acres of port, marine, and airport facilities.*

**Left, bottom:** *A freighter sits at anchor in the fog of Elliott Bay. Oil tankers and freighters carrying goods from all over the world ply the waters of Puget Sound. Arriving from the Pacific Ocean through the Strait of Juan de Fuca, the huge freighters must comply with strict speed limits once on Puget Sound; uncontrolled, their enormous wakes have caused tremendous damage to waterfront properties edging the Sound.*

**Facing page:** *Christmas-colored fishing floats lie in a colorful heap at Seattle's Fishermen's Terminal in Ballard.*

Water is Seattle's great appeal. Our family of five—and now the extended family—have an all consuming love for the water in and around Seattle. . . . Anytime we board our boat in Portage Bay we are instantly on holiday.
—Kathleen Knapp, retired

**Right, top:** *Tall enough to create its own weather system, Mount Rainier (14,411 feet) looms over Tacoma's Commencement Bay like a giant ice cream cone. Tacoma is the third largest city in Washington, stretching from lower Puget Sound east to Mount Rainier National Park. Called the "City of Destiny" after it won the bid for a railroad terminus in 1873, Tacoma is the sixth largest container port in North America and handles over 80 percent of all waterborne cargo shipped to Alaska from the lower forty-eight states. It was here in 1940 that Galloping Gertie (the original Tacoma Narrows Bridge) opened on July 1, collapsing just four months later during a wild wind storm that exacerbated its usual, undulating motion. Major restoration efforts and a growing revitalization of Tacoma's downtown area have transformed the city from an industrial rail and lumber town into a cultural hub loaded with boutiques, art galleries, restaurants, and night spots. Opened in 1983, the Tacoma Dome is the largest wood-domed arena in the world. The $40.8 million Washington State History Museum, opened in 1996, showcases the most significant collection of pioneer Native American and Alaskan artifacts on the West Coast. Scheduled for completion in 2000 is a pedestrian Bridge of Glass, which will connect the museum to the new International Museum of Glass Art, featuring the work of Tacoma-native Dale Chihuly and other famous glass artists.*

**Right, bottom:** *The Washington State Capitol Building is located in Olympia, southwest of Tacoma. Pictured here is the domed Legislative Building which was completed in 1928. The neoclassical exterior is matched by the building's opulent interior. The rotunda is faced in Alaskan tokeen marble, and large crystal chandeliers hang from the ornately painted ceilings. Statues and portraits of significant people in Washington State history have been placed throughout the building. The upper balconies of the richly decorated House and Senate chambers are also open to the public.*

**Left, top:** *The Seattle-Tacoma International Airport is located midway between the two Puget Sound cities, thirteen miles south of Seattle, sixteen miles north of Tacoma. It is owned and operated by the Port of Seattle and is served by fifty air carriers. A computer-controlled subway carries more than six hundred passengers every five minutes between the main terminal and the north and south satellites. In 1997, 24.7 million passengers passed through the airport. Sea-Tac is the closest U.S. West Coast airport to both Asia and Europe (over the North Pole)—equidistant (nine hours) between Tokyo and London.*

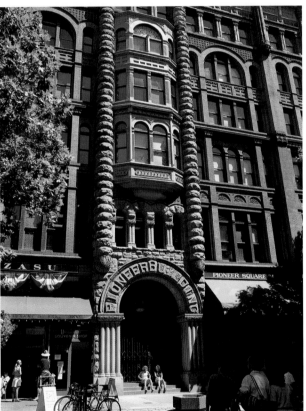

**Left, center:** *The ornate Pioneer Building, located in the heart of Pioneer Square, is one of Seattle's oldest buildings. Construction was completed after the Great Seattle Fire of June 6, 1889, which started when a glue pot spilled, igniting the wooden floor of the Pontius Building. The fire quickly spread through the fledgling wood-plank city and demolished all buildings west of Third Avenue and south of Spring Street right down to Elliott Bay. Built to last, the Pioneer Building has withstood the test of time, including a major 7.1 earthquake in 1949 that toppled its square central tower.*

**Left, bottom:** *Horse-drawn carriages add to the romantic ambiance of downtown Seattle. Rain or shine, the carriages carry lovers, families, and tourists on slow, fresh-air tours through historic Pioneer Square, around Westlake Park, and up and down the bustling Seattle Waterfront.*

**Below:** *Located in the heart of downtown Seattle, Westlake Center is popular year round, especially during the holidays. Sidewalk trees decorated with thousands of tiny white lights, a sixty-foot outdoor Christmas Tree, and a twirling, twinkling Holiday Carousel make this a festive place in December. Accessible by Monorail from the Seattle Center, the four-story Westlake Center is loaded with art galleries, restaurants, and specialty shops including a Made In Washington store and Fireworks, a regional arts and crafts gallery featuring the work of innovative Northwest artists.*

35

**Above:** *Where there's water, there are kids. The sixty-four-foot Water Wall located in front of the Westlake Center attracts young and old to this unique walk-through water sculpture. Designed by artist Robert Maki, the fluid sculpture forms a huge arch of cascading water, recreating the sound and feel of a mountain waterfall. Steel ramps provide intimate access. On a windy day, a walk through the Water Wall can definitely be a chilling experience.*

**Left:** *The Waterfall Garden Park located in Pioneer Square is a delightful place to visit. This contemplative retreat marks the spot where Jim Casey started United Parcel Service (UPS) in 1907. Ninety-one years later, UPS is now the largest package and delivery service in the world. The park was given to the people of Seattle by the Annie E. Casey Foundation in honor of the men and women of United Parcel Service. Designed by Japanese architect Masao Kinoshita, the park is one of the most expensive parks per square foot ever built in the United States. A twenty-two-foot waterfall pours five thousand gallons per minute of continuously filtered, recirculated water over massive granite slabs. This surprising little "wilderness room"—with ever-changing floral displays and thundering water tableside—is the perfect place to escape the city.*

**Left, top:** *The Boeing Company began business in this historic, two-story building in 1916. Originally used as a boathouse, William E. Boeing bought the building, called the Red Barn, and converted it into the company's first headquarters and manufacturing plant. Eighty-one years later, in 1997, Boeing booked orders for 568 commercial jetliners valued at $42.8 billion, and unveiled the first Boeing 777-300, the longest commercial jet ever built. The Red Barn is now a permanent part of the Museum of Flight, located at Boeing Field. Those eager to learn more about Boeing's early history and see planes under construction can join a free ninety-minute tour at the Boeing-Everett Tour Center in south Everett. The tour includes a movie presentation and visit to Boeing's main assembly plant, the single largest building in the world, by volume, capable of holding several 747s.*

**Left, center:** *In 1975, Microsoft cofounders Bill Gates and Paul Allen developed BASIC, the first language program written for a personal computer. They registered the name Microsoft the following year. Since then, the company has grown into the biggest personal computer software company in the world. Headquartered at their sprawling Redmond campus, Microsoft and its affluent alumni have positively influenced Seattle's local arts, education, and business scene, not to mention real estate prices. Microsoft's innovative research and development efforts continue to push the world into the high-tech future—at warp speed.*

**Left, bottom:** *The Seattle Post-Intelligencer, founded in 1863, is one of two major daily newspapers published in Seattle. This editorially spirited morning paper is owned by the Hearst Corporation. The Blethen family of Seattle owns the other, the Seattle Times. Both papers combine each week to produce a single Sunday edition. The spinning Seattle P-I rooftop globe, 30 feet in diameter with an 18.5-foot eagle perched on top, has long been a familiar city landmark.*

CHIEF SEATTLE

# The Music, History, and Art of the Emerald City

"I cannot imagine a more wonderful place to live and raise a family than
Seattle. We enjoy the nightlife, concerts, art shows, theater productions,
and sporting events of a major metropolitan area while being surrounded
by a widely varied natural wonderland. For an individual such
as myself . . . there could be no better place to call 'home.'"
—Mark Hewitt, President, Tillicum Village & Tours, Inc.

**Above:** *The Seattle Children's Theatre is a magical place for kids of all ages. Here actors Hugh Hastings
and Michael Tomkins perform a scene from the popular play,* Mr. Popper's Penguins, *on the Charlotte
Martin Theatre stage. Located in a new building near the Pacific Science Center, the Seattle Children's
Theatre encompasses two stages and an active drama school. The heartwarming selection of plays presented here delight both young and old with rich costuming and set design. They reflect artistic director
Linda Hartzell's imaginative vision for children's theatre, as well as the creative talents of Seattle's sup-
portive arts community. When the new three-story, $6 million Technical Pavillion is completed, adding
scenery, prop,and costume shops, and an entire floor of rehearsal studios, the SCT will become the most
comprehensive children's theatre in the nation.*

**Facing page:** *Artist James Wehn created this commemorative* Bust of Chief Seattle *in 1909, located
in Pioneer Square. As Chief of the Suquamish and Allied Tribes, Sealth was known as "the firm friend of
the whites," particularly to early pioneer David "Doc" Maynard. At Sealth's recommendation, Maynard
moved from Olympia in the Oregon Territory to "Duwamps" in 1852. The entrepreneurial Maynard
quickly changed the town's name to "Seattle" in honor of his Native American friend. Chief Sealth died in
1866 and was buried near the small town of Suquamish on the Kitsap Peninsula, across the Sound from
Seattle. He rests beneath two carved and painted ceremonial canoes raised high on four cedar posts.*

**Left:** *Seattle's Native American heritage is evident throughout the city in paintings and carvings depicting orcas, salmon, eagles, frogs, and bears. Totem poles are located at several locations around Seattle, including the Burke Museum, Pike Place Market, Pioneer Square, and the Seattle Center. The three-dimensional art form is closely associated with the Tlingit of southeast Alaska, the Haida of British Columbia's Queen Charlotte Islands, and the Tsimshian and Kwakiutl of coastal British Columbia. The dramatic fifty-foot totem pole standing in the middle of Pioneer Square is a replica of the one erected there in 1890. An arsonist set the original totem pole on fire in 1938; the Tlingit-carved replacement reportedly cost $5,000. Seattle's first public work of art has a checkered past. It was originally stolen from a Tlingit village in Tongass, Alaska, by a group of Seattle businessmen. The men were subsequently fined $500, but the totem pole was never returned.*

**Below:** *To enter the cathedral-like Suzzallo Reading Room at the University of Washington is to step back in time. The high, arched Gothic ceiling, carved wood bookcase relief, stained glass windows, and ornate hanging lights preserve a time long past (1926) when this room encompassed the entire collection of the University of Washington Library. Today it is just a small part of the university's library system, which includes more than twenty different libraries on and off campus. Renamed the Suzzallo Reading Room in 1991, it could well be called the Suzzallo "sleeping room," as students find the quiet room and cushioned chairs a great place to snooze away the afternoon and evening.*

Dudley Pratt sculpted twenty-eight gargoyle figures to decorate the outside of Smith Hall when it was constructed on the University of Washington campus in 1939. One of several buildings encircling the Liberal Arts Quad, Smith Hall was named after James Allen Smith who was a professor of political science from 1897 to 1924, and dean of the graduate school. Seattle University and Seattle Pacific University, both private schools, and three public community colleges are also located in Seattle.

**Above:** *Architect Steven Holl chose "A Gathering of Different Lights" as the guiding concept for his award-winning design for the Chapel of St. Ignatius at Seattle University. Completed in 1997, the exquisite chapel is an architectural masterpiece. Every square inch of the building has been crafted by local artisans with love and precision—from the combed beeswax walls to the hand-carved Alaskan yellow cedar doors and altar to the hand-blown glass pendant lights hanging from the ceiling. Holl conceived of the chapel as "seven bottles of light in a stone box," with each bottle or vessel of light corresponding to a focal aspect of Catholic worship.*

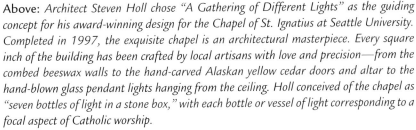

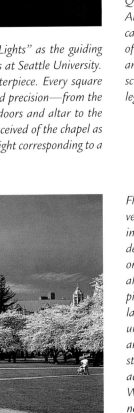

Flowering cherry trees transform the University of Washington's Liberal Arts Quad into a springtime show stopper. It is a wonderful place to picnic, stroll, read a book—or pass en route to class. The trees eventually snow petals, turning the lawns light pink. The University of Washington is the largest of Washington's five state-funded universities and colleges, with an average annual enrollment of thirty-five thousand students. The beautifully landscaped 640-acre campus touches the shores of Lake Washington and houses the university's renowned School of Medicine, College of Engineering, School of Law, and School of Business Administration. Much of the present campus is a legacy from the Alaska-Yukon-Pacific Exhibition that was held here in 1909.

Seattle's Wooden Boat Center on the south shore of Lake Union offers a unique experience: "The chance to put your hands to the oars of an eye-sweet rowboat or the tiller of a traditional wooden catboat." Described as a living museum, a skills preservation center, and a special haven on Seattle's waterfront, the Wooden Boat Center contains exhibits that aren't locked in glass cases—they float freely where they can be touched, boarded, and used. The Lake Union Wooden Boat Festival is held here each July.

Lincoln's Toe Truck is as much a Seattle fixture as the Space Needle. Here the funny pink truck appears in the International District Seafair Parade. A permanent "toe truck" is mounted at the Lincoln Towing Company lot on Mercer Street, along with their motto: "We're pulling for you, Seattle." Their delightful truck is typical of the good-natured humor of Seattleites. It is this goofball wittiness that gives the city a perpetual sense of youth and fun. Not surprisingly, the median age of Seattleites is 34.9 years, 33.7 in King County.

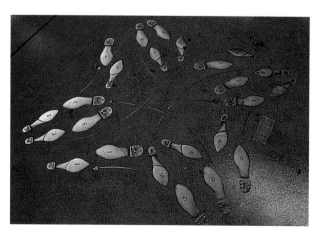

Numbered dancing feet imbedded in a sidewalk on Capitol Hill make it possible for the spontaneous to take time out for a waltz. Reflecting both Seattle's love of music and the arts and the colorful character of Capitol Hill, the bronze footprints were designed by artist Jack Mackie in 1982 as part of the "Dancer's Series" placed in eight locations along Broadway Avenue. "These dance steps came by concentrating on the people and what they do," said Mackie. "They wouldn't have worked anywhere else in the city." Capitol Hill hosts Seattle's Annual Fringe Theater Festival: seventy theatre productions, with more than 350 performances in nine Capitol Hill venues over ten days, complete with a double-decker fringe shuttle to get you there.

A bronze statue of Christopher Columbus gazes out over the harbor from Seattle's Waterfront Park. Artist Douglas Bennett created this modern sculpture of the famous explorer in 1978 to show a man who had endured a long, dangerous journey with a mutinous crew—only to discover the wrong continent. The sculpture generated a great deal of controversy when first presented to the city, due to its abstract design. After much debate, Bennett's creation was finally accepted and given a permanent place along the Seattle Waterfront.

The thirteen-ton Hammering Man *sculpture, designed by artist Jonathon Borofsky, frames the entrance to the Seattle Art Museum. Installed in 1992, the towering black silhouette—dubbed "flatman"—is made of fabricated steel, seven inches thick and forty-eight feet tall. One motor-driven arm hammers tirelessly up and down four times per minute. The Seattle Art Museum, designed by architect Robert Venturi, is considered Seattle's premiere art museum. From the entrance, visitors climb a beautiful grand staircase to rooms devoted to special changing exhibits. The large museum houses more than twenty-one thousand art objects, including permanent collections of African, contemporary, and Northwest Coast Native American art—as well as old master paintings and decorative arts from Europe, Asia, and the Americas.*

"Lightning snakes, whale-eating thunderbirds, two-headed sea serpents and animals that transform themselves into people are among the many colorful creatures that have adorned the household as well as ceremonial possessions of the Northwest Coast Indians. The dynamic imagery of these peoples, expressed in a style as rhythmic and flowing as it is complex, has created one of the world's most remarkable art traditions."
—Hilary Stewart, *Looking at Indian Art of the Northwest Coast,* 1979

It's hard to resist climbing on this inviting two-humped camel resting in front of the Seattle Asian Art Museum at Volunteer Park. The matched pair of camels frame the entrance to the renovated 1933 Art Moderne building. The building housed the original Seattle Art Museum; in 1994, the Seattle Asian Art Museum moved in, featuring the art of Japan, China, Korea, India, the Himalayas, and Southeast Asia. The reclining camels are replicas of Ming Dynasty camels from the tomb of a fifteenth-century prince. They were provided by a grant from the Seattle Foundation "for the enjoyment of the children of Seattle."

The Burke Museum of Natural History and Culture is the only major natural history museum in the United States north of San Francisco and west of the Rockies. Located on the University of Washington campus, it houses the largest collection of Pacific Northwest Native art and artifacts west of the Mississippi. The newly renovated galleries are filled with hands-on, interactive exhibits including dinosaur skeletons, a walk-through volcano, pull-out specimen drawers, and the world's only climb-inside replica of a rhino fossil. More than six hundred types of insects bejewel a clear panel "bug wall." Here is the place to gaze upon a twelve-thousand-year-old giant sloth skeleton (found at Sea-Tac Airport) or a toothy, forty-foot-long Elasmosaurus, a newly discovered marine reptile that lived here eighty million years ago.

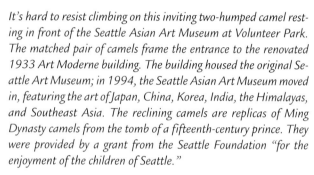

The original dragon ceiling of The 5th Avenue Theatre remains a breathtaking sight to behold. Designed by architect Robert C. Reamer, the theatre's magnificent interior was inspired by the traditional Chinese decorated wood structures of the Forbidden City and was comparable to the finest "atmospheric" theatre interiors of its time. The 5th Avenue Theatre is one of Seattle's architectural gems. Built in 1926 as a vaudeville house, The 5th Avenue served as one of the city's premier movie palaces for fifty years. The historic theatre continues to enchant all who visit. Known for its lavish set designs and inspired orchestration, The 5th Avenue produces some of the finest musical theatre entertainment in the Northwest.

**Left, top:** *Seattle's diverse music scene has been invaluably enriched by maestro Gerard Schwarz, music director of the ninety-five-year-old Seattle Symphony Orchestra. Winner of Musical America's "Conductor of the Year Award," Schwarz is internationally acclaimed for presenting elaborate symphonic concerts that showcase the work of individual composers and performing artists, especially the work of American contemporary composers. The Seattle Symphony has produced sixty-five critically acclaimed compact discs and been nominated for ten Grammy Awards. After performing at the Seattle Opera House for thirty-five years, the symphony moved in 1998 from the Seattle Center to the new Benaroya Performance Hall located in downtown Seattle. The elegant new hall features a 2,500-seat main auditorium and a 540-seat recital hall.*

**Left, center:** *Seattle is said to have more equity theatre than any U.S. city outside New York. Here, Seattle Repertory Theatre actors Sam Gregory and Jenny Bacon perform a scene from* A Doll's House. *In 1990 the Seattle Repertory Theatre won the Tony Award for Outstanding Regional Theatre. The national recognition was earned by consistently presenting the finest classic and contemporary theatre productions and by being a well-known showcase for new plays on their way to Broadway. Located on Mercer Street at the Seattle Center, the Rep has presented stage performances since 1963. All costumes and sets are created on site. Plays are performed both in the Bagley Wright Theatre and the new, adjoining Leo K. Theatre, opened in 1997. The Rep's eight-month season runs from October to May.*

**Left, bottom:** *Seattle Opera's General Director Speight Jenkins holds a costume rendering for Mozart's* Le Nozze di Figaro (The Marriage of Figaro) *while head cutter Jeffrey W. Cone works on the actual costume. Founded in 1964, Seattle Opera emphasizes opera as an art of the theatre and is most famous for its summer productions—Prokofiev's* War and Peace *during the 1990 Goodwill Games, Wagner's* Tristan and Isolde *in 1998, and the many presentations of Wagner's* Ring of the Nibelungen. *Indeed, Seattle Opera's Ring is regarded as the premier cultural and tourist event in the Pacific Northwest. The 1995 Ring presentation attracted patrons from nineteen countries and all fifty states and pumped an estimated $26 million into the local economy. A new production of Wagner's Ring is scheduled for 2001. Seattle Opera performs at the Seattle Center Opera House.*

Above: *Planes of every description fill the glassed-in Great Gallery at the Museum of Flight. Located at the south end of Boeing Field, the airy museum chronicles the history of aviation from da Vinci to the space age, including the fascinating legacy of the Boeing Company. Most popular among aviation enthusiasts are the first presidential jet (Air Force One), the world's only existing M/D-21 Blackbird and Drone Pair spy plane, and the nation's only full-sized simulated air traffic control tower. The Museum of Flight also displays a barnstorming Curtiss Jenny, a C-45 Mercy Plane (flying ambulance), and a Boeing B-47 Bomber.*

**Left:** *The Klondike Gold Rush National Historical Park is a big name for a very small park—one room in an old store in Pioneer Square (the other part of the park is located in Skagway, Alaska). However, this small museum commemorates a huge event in the history of Seattle. Gold fever hit hard on July 17, 1897, when the steamship S.S.* Portland *arrived in Seattle carrying sixty-eight passengers and more than a ton of gold. The news spread fast and one hundred thousand "stampeders" rushed to Dawson City and the Klondike gold fields between 1897 and 1898. Quick to capitalize on opportunity, Seattle made millions during the gold rush through self-promotion as the best outfitter and departure point for the Yukon. Centennial celebrations took place in 1997 to commemorate this historic event.*

"Seattle is all 'agog' with this gold fever and the streets are crowded with knots of men so worked up over the news that they can scarcely avoid being run over by the cars and carriages."
—Eugene Semple, July 17, 1897

**Top left:** *One can almost hear the wailing electric guitar of Jimi Hendrix when passing his likeness at the corner of Broadway and Pine. The life-sized bronze statue was created by Northwest artist Daryl Smith and unveiled in a "purple haze" in 1997. Born in Seattle in 1942, Hendrix was of mixed black and Cherokee ancestry. The self-taught blues and rock guitarist formed the famous rock group, The Jimi Hendrix Experience in 1966. His first album* Are You Experienced? *(1967) made him an instant star. His 1968 album,* Electric Ladyland, *became one of the most influential records of the 1960s. Hendrix died while on tour in London in 1970. He is buried at the Greenwood Cemetery in Renton.*

**Top right:** *The father and son gravesites of Bruce (1940–1973) and Brandon Lee (1965–1993) are the most frequently visited graves at Capitol Hill's Lake View Cemetery. Admirers leave behind carved jade dragons, candles, coins, flowers, and other offerings as a moving tribute to their memory. Established in 1872, this hilltop resting place has been referred to as Seattle's "pioneer cemetery" because most of the city's prominent founding families are buried here. In 1896, Princess Angeline, the daughter of Seattle's namesake, Chief Sealth, was laid to rest here in an Indian canoe, covered with a red shawl. Guided tours through this fascinating Victorian cemetery are offered by Seattle's Museum of History and Industry.*

**Right:** *Built in 1914, the forty-two-story Smith Tower was the tallest building west of the Mississippi and remained so for many years. Located near Pioneer Square, the white terra-cotta building was financed by typewriter magnate Lyman Smith to anchor Seattle's downtown area. Its priceless tile, marble, and onyx interior; Indian-head ceiling relief; and only human-operated elevators remaining on the West Coast mark an important era in Seattle history. An observation platform is located on the thirty-fifth floor. When famous seafood restaurateur Ivar Haglund owned the Smith Tower, a salmon windsock flew jauntily from the rooftop. Today the Smith Tower is dwarfed by the seventy-six-story Columbia Seafirst Center behind it.*

Frozen in bronze, Vladimir Lenin stands surrounded by guns and flames in the Fremont District. The seven-ton statue took Slavic artist, Emil Venkov, ten years to make in Poland, where it was originally installed in 1988. Lewis Carpenter, an American veteran teaching in Poland, found the toppled sculpture lying face down after the fall of the communists and the election of Solidarity in 1989. He mortgaged his home to acquire the statue and shipped it to Seattle. Vladimir Lenin is displayed in the heart of Fremont "as tangible proof that art does outlive politics"—and because it is for sale through the Fremont Chamber of Commerce—for $150,000.

Seattle was one of the first cities to pass a one-percent-for-art ordinance, which earmarks a portion of the city's budget for artistic works in public projects. As a result, the Emerald City is loaded with sidewalk art, and some of it appears in the most unexpected places. Take for instance the eight-foot-tall, Volkswagen-clutching Fremont Troll crouching under the Aurora Bridge. Its one metallic eye twinkles with rainbows in the late afternoon sun. Created by artist Steve Badanes in 1990, this climbable art is made from two tons of ferroconcrete reinforced with rebar and wire. On Halloween night—renamed "Trolloween" by the residents of Fremont—a clatter of skeleton-costumed celebrants emerges from under the bridge to lead hundreds of revelers from the home of the troll to downtown Fremont in a ghoulishly macabre march.

"I was looking for the last angry person in Seattle this past weekend. That person had apparently left. Gone to New York, Chicago, Detroit, one of those places where getting all worked up is appreciated. . . . The problem with Seattle when it's sunny and 70 degrees is that it's tough to get into a real snit. Why snit when you could be having a salmon barbecue?"
—Erik Lacitis, in "When the heat's on, people here are quite cool," *The Seattle Times,* May 20, 1997

Seattle's Fremont area is definitely a funky place; "De Libertas Quirkas" ("free to be peculiar") is the self-proclaimed neighborhood motto. This "Republic of Fremont" spirit is reflected in the eclectic shops, art galleries, brew pubs, and unique restaurants found here. A blue, fifty-three-foot-tall "Republic of Fremont Rocket," complete with neon laser pods, rises from the roof of the Bitter's Building. The rocket—along with an inscription on the Fremont Bridge—officially declares Fremont "The Center of the Universe."

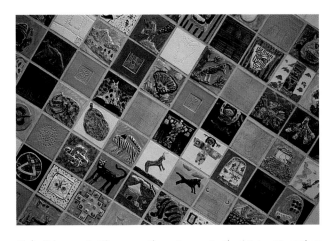

Colorful ceramic tiles cover the entrance to the Metro Tunnel at the International District Station. Created in 1989 by fourth grade students at Beacon Hill Elementary School and by fourth and fifth grade students in the bilingual program at Bailey Gatzert Elementary School, the tiles depict images from stories by and about Native American, Chinese, Japanese, Korean, Philippine, Mexican, African, and Southeast Asian people. Seattle's Metro Transit system was voted the best in the country in 1983 and 1991 by the American Public Transit Association. Between 4 A.M. and 9 P.M. it is possible to ride Seattle's downtown buses for free in a twenty-block Ride Free Zone. The 1.3-mile Metro Transit Tunnel was completed in 1990. Built beneath downtown Seattle from the Washington Trade and Convention Center to the International District, the tunnel moves more than thirty-one thousand people through the city each day. Three underground bus terminals are located in the tunnel. Each one is decorated with commissioned art work, making the tunnel as much a tourist attraction as a quick way to get around town.

Art inspires art. Waiting for the Interurban is undoubtedly one of the most popular sculptures in Seattle. Created by artists Richard Beyer and Peter Larsen in 1979, the six aluminum figures are routinely decorated for every possible holiday and special occasion. This ever-changing expression of art over a backdrop of immobile metal figures reflects the fertile humor and creativity of Fremont residents. Public works of art are located throughout the greater Seattle area—as sidewalk sculptures, wall murals painted on the outside of buildings, and cascading fountains. Renton's artistic sewage treatment plant is camouflaged as a public "waterworks garden," with winding stone mosaic paths, native plants, and serene ponds. The town of Kirkland, on the eastern edge of Lake Washington, shares sidewalk space with oversized rabbits, a life-sized cow with a coyote howling from its back, and a group of gleeful children running toward the shore—all in bronze.

The 1962 World's Fair was a special time in Seattle's history. The "Century 21 Exposition" provided an opportunity to showcase the city while getting an enhanced civic center and new and refurbished buildings. Not only did the event energize Seattle, transforming her from the pioneering Queen City of old to the new progressive Emerald City, but the 1962 World's Fair finally put Seattle on the world map. The futurist buildings designed for the Expo marked a turning point in Seattle's architecture, and its evolution into a world-class city. Soon to be added to the Seattle Center's seventy-four-acre campus will be the Pacific Science Center's "white fiberglass orb rising out of a glass box"  the new Boeing IMAX Theater, and Paul G. Allen's Experience Music Project, a 130,000-square-foot interactive museum. Designed by architect Frank O. Gehry, the museum has been described as a psychedelic rocket ship that crashed to Earth. It will open in 1999.

# The Spectacular Northwest: Nature at Its Finest

"As one who grew up within sight of the Cascades and later endured the emptiness of midwestern horizons, I find that it is the vision of summits and shoulders, notches and tarns, lake basins and sedge-filled meadows that characterizes Washington for me . . . It has been on the slopes and summits of mountains that I have best understood myself."
—Robert U. Steelquist, *Washington Mountain Ranges,* 1986

**Above:** *The Pacific Northwest offers hikers infinite possibilities for outdoor adventure. With two major mountain ranges, hundreds of lakes and glacier-melt rivers, large state and national parks, and thousands of miles of wilderness coastline, the region begs to be explored. Hiking trails weave through Douglas fir forests and lupine mountain meadows, parallel pristine rivers, and lead to the remote, wave-scoured beaches edging Puget Sound and the Pacific Ocean. One of the best ways to enjoy this beautiful Northwest wilderness is on a Mountaineers outing. Founded in Seattle in 1906, the fifteen-thousand-member Mountaineers Club has established a tradition of active volunteer leadership. The Mountaineers helped to create Olympic National Park in the 1930s and the Alpine Lakes Wilderness Area in the 1970s.*

**Facing page:** *Washington may be called the Evergreen State, but many people compare the vibrant autumn color seen here to that of New England. Dropping temperatures turn vine maples bright red and orange while other trees turn eye-shocking yellow. Such spectacular foliage displays make fall one of the best times for scenic drives throughout Washington State. The North Cascades Highway, which winds through what has been called "the American Alps," is especially popular this time of year.*

**Above:** *Canoeing is a favorite pastime on the many waterways of Western Washington. Here, a couple has rented a boat from the University of Washington Waterfront Activities Center to canoe across the Montlake Cut (a ship canal connecting Lake Union with Lake Washington) to the idyllic waters of Seattle's Washington Park Arboretum. During such a summer paddle it is possible to pick wild blackberries growing at water's edge as Canada geese tag along to mooch for picnic handouts.*

**Left:** *Autumn colors enhance the year-round beauty of the Japanese Garden at the Washington Park Arboretum. Built in 1960, the garden contains granite boulders from the Cascade Mountains and thousands of plants arranged to represent diverse scenes found in Japan. Designed by Juki Iida, every irregularly placed stone and shrub holds special meaning. Visitors should tread softly, as displacement of any item in the garden will destroy what Japanese garden scholars call niwa—or purity.*

**Facing page:** *Tulips explode with springtime color at the Washington Park Arboretum. The Arboretum also features rhododendrons, azaleas, camellias, dogwoods, and flowering cherry trees. Well-groomed trails meander through the park, across Frisbee lawns, to picnic spots and past quiet ponds. This two-hundred-acre park is one of Seattle's 397 city parks and open areas that encompass 6,189 acres, or about 10 percent of the city's total land area. Managed by both the University of Washington and the Seattle Department of Parks and Recreation, the Arboretum is landscaped with more than five thousand varieties of plants. "Tree cheers for the Arboretum!"*

**Left, top:** *A gaggle of baby geese follow an adult bird at Seward Park, Seattle's popular biking and walking spot just off Lake Washington Boulevard. Surrounded on three sides by Lake Washington, this peninsula-shaped park is encircled by a paved waterfront biking path. Seattle is loaded with urban wildlife, and Canada geese are a common sight throughout the city. Resting on docks, floating at shoreline, and grazing on park lawns and golf courses, they honk in highly vocal V-formations as they fly overhead.*

**Left, center:** *The Volunteer Park Conservatory located on Seattle's Capitol Hill, is a plant-lover's paradise. Contained inside are lush, ceiling-high tropical plants, including lemon and banana trees; orchids of every description; and sensitive plants that fold to the touch. One wing contains a goldfish pond surrounded by lush vegetation, another a desert room filled with a profusion of cactus. Open since 1912, the Conservatory is a wonderful place to visit on a rainy day.*

**Left, bottom:** *Summertime in Seattle is blackberry heaven; the plump berries grow everywhere in and around the city. While the vines can be a nuisance at times, the picking is good. Buckets of berries are turned into pies, cobblers, ice cream, and jams during this annual summer ritual. More than fifty-five thousand people attend the popular Blackberry Festival held in Bremerton each August.*

"It is hard to imagine life getting better than living in Seattle and having so many incredible places to go in less than one hour flying time from home."
—Jan W. Wagner, entrepreneur and pilot

"My city backyard hosts a surprising variety of creatures: pond-dwelling damselfly nymphs, darting Red Admirals, slinking raccoons. I sometimes glance up and view an eagle or great blue heron gliding toward Green Lake. Where else could I possibly want to live!"
—Claire Hagen Dole, Publisher, *Butterfly Gardeners' Quarterly*

**Right, top:** *Part of growing up in and around Seattle means poking through the Puget Sound tideflats. Neap tides bring out beachcombers and clam diggers in hordes. Rocks adorned with barnacles, mussels, and colorful starfish are a common sight at low-tide. Tidepool explorations can reveal the most extraordinary creatures, including chitons; green anemones; feisty, darting sculpins; and delicate sea slugs.*

**Right, bottom:** *Kayakers enjoy a sunny afternoon paddle along Seattle's ship canal. Sea kayaking is popular in the Pacific Northwest. The nationwide sport was launched here, in part, to explore the beauty of Puget Sound and the San Juan Islands. The Sound, equivalent to an inland sea, encompasses two thousand miles of coastline, twenty-four river systems, and thirteen major estuaries. Kayakers in Washington State created the Cascadia Marine Trail, a network of water trails and shoreside campsites that extends from Olympia to the San Juan Islands. The ultimate goal is to continue the trail north all the way to Skagway, Alaska. It is possible to rent kayaks at Lake Union and along the Seattle Waterfront, and guided sea kayaking tours are available throughout the San Juan Islands, including trips to see the orcas.*

Bald eagles are frequently sighted around greater Seattle. During winter, hundreds of the migratory birds congregate along the Skagit River near Marblemount to feed on spent salmon. The overwintering eagles and their habitat are protected within the Skagit River Bald Eagle Preserve. For many years, Seattle's Woodland Park Zoo has successfully rehabilitated bald eagles and other birds of prey that have been injured in the wild. Here, one such eagle poses for a portrait.

Outdoor enthusiasts take on the powerful, class-five hydraulics of the Skykomish River with a raft and paddles. Washington State offers some of the best whitewater rafting in the country on rivers that include the Elwha, Suiattle, Sauk, Tieton, White Salmon, Wenatchee, Klickitat, and Methow. Wet suits are recommended as the glacier-melt rivers can be cold, even during summer.

Built in 1881, the picturesque West Point Lighthouse is located on the western edge of Seattle's Discovery Park overlooking Puget Sound and Shilshole Bay. It is accessible by a mile-long trail that runs along the north side of the park. The 534-acre park is Seattle's largest, encompassing eight miles of beach and forest trails, nesting bald eagles, an Army fort, and the Daybreak Star Indian Cultural Center. Described as a wildlife oasis in the big city, the park attracts thousands of visitors each year—to jog, picnic, fly kites, birdwatch, beachwalk, and to just hangout with nature.

Snoqualmie Falls, located fifteen miles east of Bellevue, is a sacred site for the Snoqualmie tribe or "fierce people," once the most powerful and feared tribe in the Puget Sound region. In August 1997, the federal Bureau of Indian Affairs finally granted the Snoqualmie people tribal status after a 140-year battle to gain federal recognition. During heavy rains the Snoqualmie River floods, sending water thundering over the 268-foot falls. Puget Power operates the hydroelectric plant built in 1898 inside the rock wall behind the falls—the world's first underground electric-generating plant. Romantic Salish Lodge, perched on the rock precipice overlooking the falls, was the setting for the quirky television series Twin Peaks, filmed here during the early 1990s.

Mount Rainier reflects the glory of a summer sunset in the mirrored surface of Eunice Lake in Mount Rainier National Park. The 235,400-acre park became America's fifth national park in 1899. With more than three hundred miles of trails, the park is a hiker's dream. The ninety-three-mile Wonderland Trail completely circles the 14,411-foot mountain, crossing snowfields, streams, old-growth forests, and eleven major lava ridges for an elevation fluctuation totalling 20,500 feet. A guide service is available to lead mountain climbers to the summit. For those less energetic, Sunrise (6,400 feet) is the highest spot in the park accessible by car, as are the beautiful flower meadows of Paradise. But don't let the pretty flowers fool you: Paradise also holds the world's record for most snowfall in a season, 93.5 feet in 1972. Seattle's mascot volcano has not always been called Mount Rainier. The Puyallup and Nisqually tribes called it Tacobet, meaning "Mother of Waters."

A frog peeks out of a mushroom on the Olympic Peninsula. The Pacific Northwest has been affectionately called the land of mold spores and mushrooms, and for good reason. The damp, maritime climate, frequently cloudy skies, and abundant forests provide the ideal habitat for ferns, moss—and fungus. Mushrooms of every description grow in profusion here and set off a veritable harvesting stampede through the woods each fall. Novice collectors are warned to be careful, as there is no antidote for mushroom poisoning, and several deadly species are easily confused with the edible ones. The best place to learn more about edible fungus is at the Wild Mushroom Exhibit sponsored by the Puget Sound Mycological Society each October. The exhibit showcases more than three hundred varieties of Puget Sound—area mushrooms that are gathered and carefully labeled two days before the event. Included are species with names like Hideous Gomphidius, Witch's Butter, Dung Dome, and Dead Man's Head.

Squirrels are entertaining residents of the Pacific Northwest. These fluffy-tailed rodents are a common sight, scampering throughout Seattle's yards and parks and digging up bulbs in gardens. Western gray squirrels are the native species; the Eastern gray and fox squirrels were introduced. At night, the soft-furred, big-eyed northern flying squirrels glide between tree trunks on extended, furry, skin membranes.

**Above:** *The Skagit Valley daffodil fields paint hundreds of acres bright yellow each spring. The area's Dutch heritage is evident in the bulb and dairy farms—and the occasional windmill—found here. In April, Mount Vernon hosts the annual Skagit Valley Tulip Festival. More than fifteen hundred acres of tulips turn the ground brilliant shades of yellow, purple, red, orange, pink, and white. The vivid colors have been compared to an explosion in a paint factory. During the festival, skydivers hold hands to drop in flower formations over the fields. Families on bicycles pedal the flower-edged country lanes, and others climb out of tour buses and cars, eager for a stroll through this springtime color extravaganza.*

**Left:** *Majestic Mount Shuksan (9,127 feet) is one of several peaks that dominate the scenic North Cascades National Park. In 1859, surveyor Henry Custer wrote, "nowhere do the mountain masses and peaks present such strange, fantastic, dauntless and startling outlines as here." Encompassing five hundred thousand acres, North Cascades National Park is part of a much larger wilderness area that includes Mount Baker, Ross Lake, and Lake Chelan National Recreation Areas; Okanogan, Wenatchee, and Mount Baker–Snoqualmie National Forests; and British Columbia's Manning Provincial Park. Of the estimated 1,100 glaciers identified in the Lower 48, roughly 750 are found in this region. A road linking the east and west sides of this rugged part of the Cascade Range was completed in 1972. Since then, the beautiful North Cascades Highway (Washington SR 20) has remained open each year until winter snowfall and avalanches close the pass.*

**Left, top:** *A pair of great horned owls pose at Northwest Trek Wildlife Park. The 635-acre park is located in Eatonville, fifty-five miles southeast of Seattle on land donated by Dr. David and Connie Hellyer. As they envisioned, wildlife native to the Pacific Northwest is featured here, including wolves, grizzly bears, lynx, bobcats, and cougars. Naturalist-guided tram tours through the park, five miles of nature trails, and the Cheney Discovery Center for children make this a great year-round place to take the family. A Slug Festival, complete with slug races and the All-Slime Slug Parade, takes place here in July.*

**Left, bottom:** *The rhododendron is Washington's official state flower. From late winter to early summer, red, pink, purple, white, yellow, and blue rhododendrons bloom in profusion throughout the Northwest. One of the best places to see these spectacular blossoms each spring, if not in every local garden, is at the Washington Park Arboretum. The Weyerhaeuser Rhododendron Garden in Federal Way is also worth a visit, and each May, Port Townsend sponsors a gala weekend Rhododendron Festival.*

**Facing page:** *On May 18, 1980, Mount St. Helens surprised the world with a major north slope avalanche and lateral volcanic eruption that drastically changed two hundred square miles of forest and recreation land and killed fifty-seven people. A deadly blast of hot gas, ash, and rock particles traveling at 300 mph leveled 150,000 acres of timber like matchsticks. The avalanche triggered mudflows and flooding, and raised the once-picturesque Spirit Lake by more than two hundred feet. The pyroclastic flows reached temperatures of eight hundred degrees Fahrenheit, and the mudflows traveled more than seventy-five miles. During the eruption, an ominous gray ash cloud rose fifteen miles into the air. Today, Mount St. Helens National Volcanic Monument is one of the most interesting places to visit in the country. There are hiking trails with summer accessibility to the east side of the volcano, five different visitors centers, and a new scenic road into the monument on the west side. Nearby Ape Cave can be explored on foot with lanterns. The cave is the longest intact lava tube (12,810 feet) in the continental United States. An excellent film about the eruption is shown at the new Johnston Ridge Observatory. The observatory, opened in 1997, is named in memory of volcanologist David Johnston who was killed while standing on this ridge. Announcing the start of the eruption, his last words were, "Vancouver. Vancouver. This is it!"*

**Left:** *Sol Duc Falls and Hot Springs in Olympic National Park are wonderful places to recharge one's urban batteries. Located near magnificent Lake Crescent along the northern part of the Olympic Peninsula, the Sol Duc area offers groomed hiking trails that weave through the moss-draped cathedral forests and over rustic log bridges. A one-mile trail takes visitors from a roadside parking lot to the rainbowed mist of the forty-foot Sol Duc Falls. Further down the road is the entrance to the Sol Duc Hot Springs Resort where overnight guests and day-visitors can soak away their cares in sulfured water that reaches temperatures of 106 degrees Fahrenheit. Further west along Highway 101, travelers can get soaked another way by visiting Forks, Washington, one of the wettest places in the continental United States. In 1997, just under thirteen feet of rain fell on this peninsula town.*

"When I was growing up my family would drive over Stevens Pass several times a year. Near the summit, rain or not, we would get out of the car and walk a short way into the woods. 'Breathe deeply,' Dad would say. 'Feel that air? It's different here!'"
—Helen Freeman, Chair/Founder,
International Snow Leopard Trust

**Above:** *A fiery sunset engulfs the Lime Kiln Lighthouse on the west side of San Juan Island. Built in 1919, the lighthouse is part of Lime Kiln Point State Park, also known as Whale Watch Park. The lighthouse warns boats in Haro Strait away from the hazardous rocks at shoreline and serves as an ideal lookout for passing pods of orcas. As many as seventy orcas have passed this point in a single day. San Juan Island is one of 172 picturesque islands—many more if you count them at low tide—in the San Juan archipelago. A fun way to explore this fifty-seven-square-mile island is by moped, which can be rented, along with bicycles, in the town of Friday Harbor.*

**Left:** *A fresh blanket of snow covers Hurricane Ridge in winter white. This popular hiking, snowshoeing, and cross-country skiing destination is part of Washington's Olympic National Park. The ridge is accessible by road from Port Angeles, "from sea level to ski level within thirty minutes." At 5,240 feet, Hurricane Ridge offers a panoramic view of the Olympic Mountains and Canada across the Strait of Juan de Fuca. Olympic National Park is one of Washington's most beautiful parks. Encompassing temperate rain forests, rugged Pacific Ocean beaches, and the Olympic Mountains, this three-in-one park requires several days to explore.*

Mount Rainier is framed by the scenic town of Gig Harbor at the southern end of Puget Sound, thirty miles south of Seattle. This postcard-perfect scene—boats, snow-capped peaks, evergreen forests, and beautiful sunrises and sunsets—is repeated throughout the Puget Sound area at the many small marinas that edge the inlets and islands of the Sound and the San Juans.

A pod of orcas surfaces near Lime Kiln Point on San Juan Island. For years, marine biologists at the Friday Harbor Whale Museum have studied the feeding and ranging behavior of the separate family groups, or pods, found in these waters. The distinctive black-and-white orcas appear frequently in the art and legends of the Pacific Northwest Native Americans. Their likeness also appears printed on regional buses, trucks, mailboxes, signs, banners, and in enormous wall murals painted on several Seattle buildings. Whale-watching trips to see the beloved orcas can be arranged through the Seattle Aquarium, Mosquito Fleet, and Friday Harbor Whale Museum. But one of the most exciting ways to see an orca is from a sea kayak.

Brightly clothed birders use binoculars and scopes to spy on the migratory flocks of sandpipers that gather each winter at Bowerman Basin near Hoquiam, Washington. Up to one million shorebirds, mostly western sandpipers, gather on the muddy tideflats of the Grays Harbor estuary each spring. Located in the middle of the Pacific Flyway for numerous species of migratory birds, Washington State is a haven for birdwatchers. More than 150 species of birds, including backyard songbirds and species that use freshwater habitats, make the long flight from Latin America to the Pacific Northwest each year. An estimated twenty-seven thousand snow geese annually travel three thousand miles from Russia's Wrangel Island in the East Siberian Sea to overwinter on Fir Island in Skagit County. Trumpeter swans from the north congregate during winter in the Skagit Valley, and bald eagles gather by the hundreds along the Skagit River.

The rugged Washington coast, washed by the Pacific Ocean, is undeveloped compared to the Atlantic coast. Wild winter storms have left the shores log strewn and the rocks sculpted, occasionally washing up glass fishing floats that have drifted on currents all the way from Japan. Ruby Beach, located within Olympic National Park, is a wonderful place to beachcomb, especially after a winter storm. This is nature at its best, untamed, unchanged, and surf-pounding wild. If you linger 'til sunset, it is also the perfect place to look for the elusive "green flash"—an optical illusion where the sun appears to turn green just as it dips below the horizon.

# A City Celebrates:
# Festivals and Fairs

"I'll never leave the Seattle area; it will always be my home."
—Wendy Skony, Environmental Coordinator for the City of Bellevue

**Above:** *The Seattle Seafair Clowns pose for their official Seafair photo at Kerry Park on Queen Anne Hill. It is probably the most stationary this raucous group ever gets during their three weeks of high-energy parades, photo shoots, and guest appearances all over the city. Such clowning around is all part of the high spirited fun of Seattle's annual Seafair celebrations held each summer. The colorful Seafair Clowns are an important part of this tradition, entertaining folks wherever their Clown Mobile may wander.*

**Facing page:** *A little girl in a festive kimono helps to celebrate the Bon Odori Festival. Sponsored by the Betsuin Buddhist Temple every July in Seattle's International District, this colorful Asian celebration reenacts an ancient Japanese ritual that dates back to the tenth century. As the Gateway to Asia in trade, commerce, and physical proximity, Seattle is home to a large Asian population. The best place to experience this rich cultural legacy is in Seattle's large International District, located just east of Union Station. Don't miss a visit to Uwajimaya, the large Japanese supermarket, bazaar, and delicatessen that sells everything from live sea cucumbers to fresh sushi and hot dim sum (Chinese appetizers). During Chinese New Year celebrations, sidewalks in the International District literally turn red with firecracker wrappers.*

"More than any other area in the United States, the Northwest has a splendor and peacefulness that is apparent in almost every one of its localities. And along with the beauty of nature's handiwork, the people here have style and attitude that are quietly conducive to intimacy and affection. A Northwest secret is, the more intimately acquainted you are with the earth, the more intimate you can be with each other. In short, it is not only better to kiss here, it is sheer ecstasy."
—Paula Begoun, *The Best Places to Kiss in the Northwest: A Romantic Travel Guide,* 1997

*A sword swallower mesmerizes a crowd at Seattle's Northwest Folklife Festival. Each year more than 225,000 people attend this four-day event in May, hailed by many as Seattle's most important cultural event. More than one thousand music and dance performances from more than one hundred different countries appear on eighteen stages during the festival. The performances include Eastern European line dances, African marimbas, Scandinavian hambos, and Native American storytellers.*

*The Fourth of July gets Seattle revelers out early in anticipation of the big pyrotechnic event. Large fireworks displays are lit off simultaneously at 10:00 P.M. at two downtown locations: the AT&T Family Fourth at Lake Union and the Fourth of Jul-Ivar's at Myrtle Edwards Park near Pier 71. Here pleasure boats have dropped anchor in Elliott Bay, and landlubbers have staked out their turf at Myrtle Edwards Park to enjoy live music on three stages, a flyover of antique planes sponsored by the Museum of Flight, culminating with a spectacular pyroplastic display.*

*From roots to rooflines, Seattle is a musical city, and there is no better place to witness this melodious exuberance than outside during summertime. Street musicians of every description play their instruments and sing, entertaining appreciative crowds at the Seattle Center, Westlake Center, and the Pike Place Market. There is even a couple called the "Ferryboat Musicians" that sing and play guitars for passengers on the Washington State Ferries.*

A Seattle Seafair Pirate holds a willing captive at sword point during the pirates' boisterous, weapon-waving landing at Alki Beach. The notorious "pirates" take great pride in "scaring" little kids and "kidnapping" fair maidens during their citywide appearances each summer. Such swashbuckling fun is all part of the annual Seafair celebrations, which include neighborhood parades, Seafair clowns, pirates, and the big Torchlight Parade. Seattle's summer blast concludes with the thundering Seafair Unlimited Hydroplane Races on Lake Washington, highlighted by a spectacular U.S. Navy Blue Angels Air Show performed right over the race course.

An all-girl drill team shows off their pretty costumes and polished marching skills during the International District Seafair Parade. Many different cultures are featured during this annual summer parade. Most popular is the appearance of the dazzling, one-hundred-foot-long Chinese dragon that requires one hundred men to maneuver as its brightly colored body undulates through the streets. The dragon was a gift to the International District from Seattle's sister city, Kaohsiung, Taiwan.

Who says Seattleites don't know how to have fun? At the annual Seafair Milk Carton Derby on Green Lake, jubilant contestants design and construct their hilarious "moo" crafts out of paper and plastic milk jugs. Participants are judged not only on the speed with which they finish the race course, but on their creative use of construction materials and the ability to stay afloat. Anyone "got milk?"

Enticing aromas, colorful banners, live music, and lots of great eats attract thousands of people to the Millstone Coffee Bite of Seattle each July. The 1996 Events Business News rated this festival number seven out of the top two hundred events held throughout the country. Held at the Seattle Center, nearly four hundred thousand people attend the huge weekend food festival, making it one of the best eating and people-watching events of the summer. It's definitely the place to go with a big appetite. Here's your chance to try everything from elephant ears and Indian fry bread tacos to Biringer Farm's famous strawberry shortcake. More than one hundred menu items are offered at over fifty participating restaurant stands.

Tugboats play a vital role in maneuvering freighters in and out of the Seattle harbor. They can weigh up to eight hundred tons, have two eighteen-cylinder diesel engines, produce five thousand horsepower, and pull sixty tons. Therefore, the concept of a tugboat race seems like an oxymoron. Yet, race they do. Tugboat racing, in one form or another, has been part of Seattle's history since there were tugs. Here a group of tugboats cut loose on Elliott Bay during the Seattle Maritime Festival in May. The tugs churn up the water at 15 to 18 mph over the 2.2-mile course. A parade of harbor tugs with tires for bumpers, oceangoing tugs, classic refitted tugs, and pleasure tugs with wet bars are all part of the day's fun.

Seattle has a large, highly visible, highly vocal gay community. More than thirty gay clubs and bars are located on and off Broadway on Capitol Hill. In addition to a remarkable tolerance for religious and ethnic differences, Seattleites show a similar acceptance of most gender issues. In addition to gay cruises, there is the annual Halloween Costume Ball called "Bump in the Night." A gay parade held in Seattle the last weekend in June attracts seventy thousand people each year, making it the second largest parade in the city after the Torchlight Parade. Big-name bands, such as Seattle-based The Presidents of the United States of America, play at the annual Chicken Soup Brigade Dance-athon.

Live music, entertainment, and spontaneous street performances draw fifty thousand people a day to the Fremont Street Fair each June. This is the time to see Fremont at its funkiest, especially during the annual Solstice Parade, which includes clowns, musicians, steel drummers, and fifteen or more people-powered, homemade floats. Organizers describe the fair as a parade in itself, as participants join in to sing, dance, and paint their faces. The only rules in this bohemian event involve the parade: no printed words or logos, no animals, and no motors. Otherwise this dog-friendly fair is a great place to test your spontaneous artistic talents, graze the food booths, sip a latte, and, in general, just hang out, people-watch, and enjoy a warm summer day.

Thrillseekers ride a roller coaster at the Western Washington Fair in Puyallup. Billed as the largest fair on the West Coast, "the Puyallup Fair" is held every September. This is the place to blow your diet on Fisher's famous hot raspberry scones, hot buttered corn, barbecue ribs, and the fair's famous grilled onion cheeseburgers. The Double Arch Rocket Launcher, Bungee Jump, Ejection Seat, and Extreme Swing provide screamable thrills for the young at heart. For those less interested in zero-gravity experiences, there are livestock exhibits, pig races, poultry and rabbit shows, quilt displays, celebrity shows, a rodeo—and more food booths to sample. During the final week of the 1997 Puyallup Fair, one thousand fluttering monarch butterflies were released en masse.

Above: *The Bubble Man, "edutainer" Garry GoLightly, delights young and old alike with his fragile, shimmering creations at the Northwest Folklife Festival. During thirteen years of blowing bubbles, GoLightly has traveled to thirty countries, appearing on game shows in Tokyo and at festivals in Australia. GoLightly considers Seattle bubble heaven. "The reason I moved here," he says, "is because Seattle has the perfect bubble weather—cool, calm and cloudy." The Northwest Folklife Festival, one of the region's major ethnic and traditional arts events, is held at the Seattle Center each May. It helps kick-off a summer-long series of festivals and celebrations held throughout the city.*

Facing page: *A young Native American dancer peeks through eagle feathers and beadwork at the annual Seafair Indian Days Pow Wow held at the Daybreak Star Arts and Cultural Center in Discovery Park. Each year, more than four thousand Native Americans from nine states and Canada gather to sing, dance, drum, and chant during this three-day event. The Duwamish and Suquamish tribes were the original settlers of Puget Sound. Semi-nomadic, they relied on seasonal harvests of plants and hunted available game. The Duwamish lost their land with the signing of the Point Elliott Treaty in 1855. Because they were not given their own reservation land in this treaty agreement, the government still does not officially recognize the Duwamish as a tribe.*

*Crowds watch as a bucking bronco prepares to throw its spurred rider onto the ground. During summer, rodeos are held at numerous towns throughout the Pacific Northwest, including Chelan, Toppenish, Newport, Long Beach, and Colville. The Ellensburg Rodeo, one of the biggest, is held in August as part of the Kittitas County Fair. This granddaddy of Washington State rodeos attracts more than twenty-seven thousand people each year.*

"OK, we all know Seattleites love their coffee and their dogs. Hikes, neighborhood walks, and day trips are commonplace for most of us, with a cup of joe in one hand and the leash of you-know-who in the other."
—Ranny Green,
*The Seattle Dog Lover's Companion*, 1996

**Left, top:** *Dressed in colonial attire, a woman displays a collection of vintage rifles at the annual Heritage Festival. The festival is held every July in Redmond's Marymoor County Park. This eclectic event features everything from Civil War reenactments, mountain man demonstrations of survival skills, and Native Americans carving totem poles to Greek dancing, bluegrass fiddle music, and Tibetan monks performing sacred music and dance.*

**Left, center:** *Kissing goats is just part of the fun at the annual King County Fair held each July in Enumclaw. Nestled among dairy farms and white-fenced thoroughbred farms that breed race horses for competition at Emerald Downs Race Track, Enumclaw is located forty-four miles from Seattle—the self-proclaimed gateway to Mount Rainier and excellent winter skiing at Crystal Mountain. A loggers' show, rodeo, and big name entertainment add color to this regional summer fair.*

**Left, bottom:** *"The Sisters of Perpetual Indulgence" mug for the camera during the University District Street Fair. This light-hearted group of guys dresses in drag and makes drop-in appearances at clubs, restaurants, and public events throughout Seattle. Such uninhibited, free-spirited fun is typical of Seattle, where it is possible to see a giant inflated crab hanging from the Space Needle, a dog riding on the back of a motorcycle, or people dancing in the street to a calypso band.*

**Above:** *A scenic drive over Stevens Pass through the Cascade Mountains leads to the quaint little town of Leavenworth. Designed to resemble a Bavarian village in Germany, this delightful town is a great place to spend a day, or weekend, with excellent shopping and a variety of restaurants. The town hosts several gala celebrations throughout the year, including the Autumn Leaf Festival, Bavarian Ice Fest, Christmas Lighting Festival, and the International Folk Dance Festival. Leavenworth is a fun, atmospheric spot to sip hot-spiced wine and munch a bratwurst after skiing or snowboarding at Stevens Pass.*

*Seattle is a city of dog lovers. The pampered pets ride the Washington State ferries, cruise Puget Sound on luxury yachts, go fishing for salmon and trout, and prance on leashes in Emerald City parks (though uninhibited romping is allowed in select, leash-free parks). Here a Boston terrier in a baby sling sports a matching playsuit and visor crafted by a vendor at the University District Street Fair. The popular spring fair hosts artists and food vendors from all over the Northwest.*

*Artists and art collectors alike turn out by the thousands to enjoy the more than three hundred juried craft booths, continuous performing arts shows, and visual arts exhibits at the Pacific Northwest Arts Fair. Held in late July at Bellevue Square, the three-day extravaganza is the largest outdoor arts and crafts event in the Northwest. Upscale Bellevue, the fourth largest city in Washington State, is connected to Seattle by two floating bridges that span Lake Washington.*

# The Northwest Lifestyle

"I'm here for the weather. Well, yes, I'm also here for the volcanoes and the salmon, and the exciting possibility that at any moment the volcanoes could erupt and pre-poach the salmon. I'm here for the rust and the mildew, for webbed feet and twin peaks, spotted owls and obscene clams (my consort says I suffer from geoduck envy), blackberries and public art (including that big bad mural the authorities had to chase out of Olympia), for the ritual of the potlatch and the espresso cart, for bridges that pratfall into the drink and ferries that keep ramming the dock."
—Tom Robbins, author, from "Why I Live in Northwestern Washington"

*Above: In Seattle, umbrellas are a colorful art form unto themselves. While most natives forego bothering with the temperamental contraptions—or just simply lose them—a few insist on doing battle with the region's gusty showers. At the end of a good storm, city trash bins overflow with the skeletons of spent umbrellas, their spokes twisted into a myriad artistic shapes. In spite of its reputation, Seattle ranks forty-fourth in a listing of U.S. cities by rainfall amounts. The Emerald City has less rain each year than Atlanta, Houston, Boston, New York, Philadelphia, and Washington, D.C., averaging 36.2 inches a year.*

*Facing page: A neon coffee sign, complete with twisting wisp of steam, is mounted enticingly at the entrance to Post Alley at the Pike Place Market. Seattle has been called a city of lattes and rain, and owners of espresso stands and coffee houses often claim that there is a correlation between caffeine consumption rates and precipitation. Apparently, they both increase together.*

**Above:** *Seattle is famous for fresh seafood, especially salmon, Dungeness crab, and oysters. In fact, Washington State is the country's leading producer of oysters. These delectable treats can be air-shipped with dry ice from the Pike Place Market to just about anywhere in the United States. Tourists and residents alike make a run to the local seafood restaurants when Alaska's prized Copper River salmon is in season. Ivar's, McCormick's, Salty's, Ponti's Seafood Grill, Anthony's, Arnie's, and Ray's Boathouse are some of Seattle's best seafood restaurants.*

**Left:** *Fishermen silhouetted by sunrise line the 120-foot public fishing pier at Seacrest Park in West Seattle. Many places around the Seattle Waterfront allow public access, making it possible to drop a line—or crab trap—in some of the most scenic fishing spots imaginable. Everything from dogfish, smelt, and rock cod to salmon and Dungeness crabs are caught off the piers. In winter, Seattle anglers nightfish for squid. The Seacrest fishing pier remains open year-round, even when state fishing quotas close Elliott Bay to boat salmon fishing.*

"I feel fortunate to live in the Northwest. I have experienced fantastic and unforgettable runs along the Seattle waterfront, surrounding lakes, and the Burke-Gilman and Centennial Trails. Nothing compares to running on Queen Anne Hill and taking in the breathtaking view of downtown Seattle and the waterfront and mountains!"
—Dode Hutchinson, Aerobic Director,
Mill Creek Athletic Club

**Left., top:** *A crabber holds a Dungeness crab caught from the public fishing pier in West Seattle. These delectable crustaceans are part of Seattle's seafood legacy. Served in crab cocktails, fresh seafood salads, and stuffed in fish filets and oversized shrimp, Dungeness crabs are enjoyed in a variety of dishes. However, they are best when simply boiled, cleaned, and dipped in melted butter.*

**Left, bottom:** *The Pacific Northwest is home to some giant creatures, including the foot-long Pacific giant salamander, the thirteen-inch gum boot or Pacific giant chiton (the largest in the world), a three-pound giant barnacle, and the giant Pacific octopus—the world's largest octopus—which can weigh up to four hundred pounds with suckered appendages that stretch twenty-eight feet from tip to tip. Included in this super-size menagerie is the geoduck (pronounced "gooey duck"), one of the world's largest burrowing clams. Sporting an eight-inch shell and weighing up to twelve pounds, this giant native bivalve was once the butt of endless rude jokes, and as such, chopped unceremoniously into clam chowders. But the mega clam now fetches thirteen to twenty dollars a pound or more, and is shipped both legally and illegally to Japan where the coveted clams are in big demand. Geoducks are the number-one tideland revenue producer for the state Department of Natural Resources, whose licensing of the legal harvest brings in $6 million to $8 million annually.*

"Although I have lived in other cities for short periods of time, only Seattle feels like home. On a clear day the beauty is breathtaking, the mountains, the water and the lush green vegetation are a feast for the eyes."
—Wendy Wienker, Registrar, Woodland Park Zoological Gardens

**Right:** *Opening of the annual trout fishing season in late April is a much-anticipated event throughout the Northwest. It is a yearly ritual of midnight bonfires and cookouts, fishing derbies, and angler advice about the best bait to use and tales of the big one that got away. Here, a boy at Green Lake Park in north Seattle shows off a rainbow trout. A three-mile paved path encircles the lake, making this beloved Seattle park one of the best places to walk, jog, bike, skate, sunbathe, swim, or paddle boat.*

**Below:** *Bivalve enthusiasts take full advantage of Washington's carefully controlled clamming seasons up and down the state's beautiful Pacific Coast and Puget Sound beaches. These clammers are digging at Kalaloch Beach on the Olympic Peninsula. Limited to fifteen razor clams per day per person, licensed clammers young and old take digging seriously. Armed with hipwaders, clam guns (a specially designed clam shovel), and sacks to haul away their bivalve bounty, clammers are often up before dawn to pursue their prey, digging clams right in the surf.*

**Above:** *Colorful ships line the docks of Port Angeles, the major "gateway city" to the Olympic Peninsula and an official Port of Entry to the United States. The headquarters of Olympic National Park are located here, along with the access road to the park's Hurricane Ridge area. Victoria, British Columbia, accessible by ferry, lies just seventeen miles north of the city across the Strait of Juan de Fuca. The mighty Olympic Mountains form a dramatic backdrop to Port Angeles's charming waterfront. The spectacular mountains are best seen on a moonlit night from Ediz Hook. Billed as the second-largest sandpit in the world, Ediz Hook reaches out like a protective arm to form Port Angeles's calm-water harbor.*

**Right:** *Like a still-life painting, a sailboat rests quietly at anchor in Seattle's Elliott Bay at sunset. Beautiful summer scenes such as this explain why so many people endure Seattle's notorious "liquid sunshine" during a rainy season that often lasts from November to May. As soon as the sun comes out, the drizzle and battleship-gray clouds are quickly forgotten. Seattle's mild climate often makes it possible for a cherry tree to bloom right next to a golden maple tree that refuses to lose its autumn leaves. Located at latitude 47° north, Seattle is farther north than Bangor, Maine, which means sixteen wonderful hours of daylight during summertime.*

**Above:** *Waterfront restaurants accessible by boat, and a main street lined with art galleries, make the picturesque town of La Conner a popular, year-round tourist destination. Framed by the Cascade Mountains to the east with the 10,778-foot, glacier-covered Mount Baker rising in the background, historic La Conner is a fun town to visit, especially during the August Blues Fest, or in February when young and old turn out to "jig for smelt" during the town's annual Smelt Derby. As they say, "It takes a jerk to catch a smelt."*

**Left:** *Seattle's maritime climate makes this a great place to grow everything from mushrooms to moss. A gardener's delight, perennials usually bloom twice, once in the spring and again in the fall. Dahlia blossoms grow as big as dinner plates, and roses bedazzle in every size and color, especially at the award-winning Rose Garden at Seattle's Woodland Park Zoo, where it is possible to enjoy the fragrant blossoms while listening to twilight flute concerts. Here a West Seattle family shows their impassioned addiction to gardening by covering their eye-catching waterfront house with summer flowers.*

**Above, left:** *The movie* Sleepless in Seattle *was filmed on a houseboat very near this location on Lake Union. The modern, as well as funky, houseboats edging Lake Union, the ship canal, and Portage Bay near the Seattle Yacht Club are a local novelty. During the Fourth of July celebrations on Lake Union, houseboat residents and their guests sit on the roofs, barbecue on their balconies, and dance on the docks as hundreds of partying boaters anchor nearby. The best way to tour Seattle's quaint houseboats is, not surprisingly, by boat, preferably on a summer night when the beautiful interiors are illuminated.*

**Above, right:** *Made famous by Ivar Haglund, who encouraged customers at his Waterfront Fish Bar to "Feed the Seagulls," these squawking scavengers can be seen throughout the city. Their raucous calls are as much a part of the Seattle Waterfront scene as is the invigorating smell of salt water. Seagulls swoop down to remove food held at fingertip, even chasing the ferries across Puget Sound in hopes of a handout.*

**Right:** *Resembling a row of king salmon displayed at a fish market, the silver rental canoes at the University of Washington Waterfront Activities Center are lined up, ready for use. In addition to paddling through the lily-pond waters of the Arboretum, it is also possible to take the canoes through the Montlake Cut to Portage Bay. It is an inexpensive way to become an immediate part of Seattle's exuberant high- and low-brow boating scene.*

**Left:** *Experienced and novice rock climbers can practice various routes up the popular indoor climbing pinnacle at REI's (Recreational Equipment, Inc.) new flagship store in downtown Seattle. The sixty-five-foot climbing pinnacle is the tallest, free-standing indoor climbing structure in the world. Opened in 1996, the store is a monument to outdoor recreation. It is landscaped with a 470-foot mountain bike test trail and a rain-water-charged, recirculating waterfall that thunders near the entrance. Such dramatic features help emphasize REI's position as a leading national retailer of durable and dependable outdoor gear and clothing. REI was started as a co-op by twenty-three Seattle mountain climbers in 1938, and members of REI still receive annual dividends based on their purchases.*

**Below:** *A four-mile stretch of scenic Lake Washington Boulevard, edging the southwest shore of Lake Washington, is closed to car traffic on Bicycle Sunday. This enables cyclists of all ages and skill levels to safely bike from Mount Baker Beach to Seward Park, where riders can access two additional miles of bike trails. Seattle is bicycle-friendly with bike paths all over the city. The twelve-mile Burke-Gilman Trail skirts the shores of Lake Washington to Gas Works Park on Lake Union. Even the express lanes of Interstate 5 are occasionally closed to motorists so bikers can pedal the freeway. Each year, AT&T cosponsors the Seattle-to-Portland (STP) Bicycle Classic; more than ten thousand bikers pedal the 180 miles during the two-day event.*

**Right, top:** *Joggers enjoy the paved paths around Gas Works Park on the north shore of Seattle's Lake Union. In 1907, the Seattle Gas Company established a gas works project on the site. When the area was reclaimed as a high-density public park in 1978, the historic crackling towers were left in place and incorporated into the park's award-winning design. Gas Works Park is a great place to picnic, fly kites, and watch the Tuesday night sailboat races on Lake Union during summer. It is also the best spot, short of being on a boat, to watch the spectacular Fourth of July fireworks display choreographed over the lake.*

**Right, center:** *Like dragonflies (Washington's official state insect) seaplanes are everywhere around Seattle. They tie up to houseboats and perch in front of grand waterfront homes on Lake Washington. The pontooned planes buzz cars on the I-5 bridge, career around city buildings, and land and take off amidst kayaks and yachts on Lake Union. Kenmore Air, the world's largest seaplane operation, offers daily scheduled flights to Victoria, British Columbia, and the San Juan Islands from Lake Union. Seattle Seaplanes offers charter flights just about anywhere, including sightseeing flights around the city, quick escapes to the San Juan Islands, trips to Victoria and Vancouver, and flights to the most remote fishing lodges in western Canada—all from the heart of downtown Seattle.*

**Right, bottom:** *The CBS show* Northern Exposure *put the tiny town of Roslyn, Washington (a.k.a. Cicely, Alaska) on the map. The former coal-mining town is eighty-nine miles from Seattle, just southeast of Snoqualmie Pass. It was here that the popular television series was filmed, often in the Brick Tavern. The Roslyn Cafe continues to be a great place to eat, even if one can no longer catch a glimpse of the show's popular actors. Roslyn, remarkably, has a large number of cemeteries. Uphill from the cafe lie twenty-five different cemeteries—each one representing a different nationality of the miners who worked and died in Roslyn.*

Commuters stream back and forth across Lake Washington on the Evergreen Point Bridge, the longest floating bridge in the world. It is one of two floating bridges that connect the eastside cities of Bellevue, Kirkland, Woodinville, and Redmond with downtown Seattle. Here, strong winds whip up white-capped waves that break along the south side of the bridge. The first of the bridges was completed in 1940; until then, ferries carried passengers back and forth across the lake.

"Living in the Northwest, we are fortunate to encounter wildlife in our everyday lives," says Kathy Kelly, executive director of PAWS (the Progressive Animal Welfare Society). "Raccoons walk our backyard alleys, deer look up in surprise as we round a bend on a hiking trail, and hawks peer at us from light poles above the freeway. Occasionally, bears prowl suburban parking lots and coyotes crouch in downtown elevators." Last year alone, over five thousand wild animals came through the doors of the PAWS Wildlife Center located in Lynnwood, north of Seattle. Here, PAWS wildlife care supervisor, Jennifer Convy, checks on a barred owl, one of two hundred different species of wildlife routinely cared for and rehabilitated, if possible, at the center.

**Above left:** *The Starbucks Coffee Company, named after the java-junkie chief mate in Herman Melville's novel* Moby Dick, *was started in Seattle's Pike Place Market in 1971. Since then, the company has grown globally like a cell-division experiment on steroids. This phenomena is best seen at the Sea-Tac Airport where Starbucks latte lines are often longer than those of passengers waiting to board airplanes. There seems to be no stopping this mermaid-logoed coffee roaster as Starbucks continues to take over the world, one cup at a time.*

**Above, right:** *Yes, Seattleites do worship coffee, as "espressed" by the signs on this coffee house on Capitol Hill. In fact, it's hard to believe that one city can support as many espresso stands, coffee houses, coffee shops, and bean-grinding locations as it does, but they are everywhere. In 1997, Webster's* New World College Dictionary *included the word "latte" for the first time. According to a press release by the Macmillan Publishing company to mark the occasion, the coffee craze started by Seattle-based Starbucks was posing quite a problem for its "distinguished team of lexicographers."*

**Right:** *Seattle is the undisputed espresso capital of the world— even though the drink originated in Italy. There are more than two hundred licensed espresso stands—with names like Cup of Java, Jitters, Javabean, and Espresso A Go-Go—in the greater Seattle area, so one doesn't have to go far without a double half-caf, tall skinny latte with a shot of mango. Here, Ken Turner, owner of Coffee Messiah, enjoys a cup of the addicting elixir.*

Rainy day, rain all day.
Ain't no use in getting uptight,
Just let it groove its own way.
Let it drain your worries away;
Lay back and groove on a rainy day,
Lay back and dream on a rainy day.

—*Still Raining, Still Dreaming*
by Jimi Hendrix

The Emerald Queen *Casino is the only floating casino in the state of Washington. The Puyallup tribe operates the* Emerald Queen, *an authentic replica of a New Orleans riverboat, on Tacoma's Blair Waterway. Twenty-seven Washington State tribes are currently recognized by the federal government, and seven more have petitioned. Many of the tribes, including the Muckleshoot, Tulalip, and Swinomish have built casinos on their land. At the American Indian Heritage School in Seattle, as many as fifty different tribal affiliations are represented.*

*The Merchants Cafe in Pioneer Square is Seattle's oldest restaurant; it has "served the needs of pioneers, politicians and other scoundrels since 1890." The booths are antiques, the safe and gold scale are originals, and the thirty-foot standup bar came by schooner around Cape Horn. Hooks still visible on the outside alley walls were used to lower beer kegs into the basement. Listed on the National Register of Historic Places, the restaurant features hand-crafted ales, Northwest wines, and local seafood. Located within walking distance from the Waterfront and Kingdome, the Merchants Cafe is surrounded by art galleries, theatres, and some of the city's best nightclubs.*

*Brew pubs are popular and plentiful in the Pacific Northwest. At last count there were fifteen microbreweries in King County, forty-nine in the state. One of the best ways to tap into the microbrewery scene is to join a tour. Redhook Ale Brewery, pictured here, offers daily tours of their brewing facility and samples at the Trolleyman Pub in the Fremont District, as does nearby Hale's Ale Brewery & Pub. Pyramid Breweries in Pioneer Square and the Pike Pub and Brewery at the Pike Place Market also offer tours. It is even possible to mix your own batch of beer, bottle it, and label it at Kirkland's Northwest Brewwërks, one of several "U Brew" places around the area.*

"Seattle has a great business environment and there are many opportunities available—from the aerospace and high-tech giants to the small business entrepreneurs. One aspect of the Seattle business community is its capacity to care not only about the budget bottom line, but the value it places on the social and human condition."
—Frances Jo Carr, Executive Assistant to the Mayor, City of Seattle

**Right, top:** *Sidewalk art appears in the most unexpected places in Seattle, some of it quite spontaneous in origin. For years, the outside of the purple-and-green Jell-O Mold Building on Western Avenue was decorated with a bizarre collection of metal gelatin molds—until 1997 when it was torn down. Here, colorful wads of gum have been carefully placed on the brick wall outside the Market Theatre at Seattle's Pike Place Market. Located on crooked, cobblestoned Post Alley, this funky little theatre seems the perfect location for a "gum wall." It is the main stage for Unexpected Productions (the Cream of Wit and Seattle TheatreSports League), which specializes in improvisational theatre. Since 1991, Unexpected Productions has developed, written, and produced thirty shows, including Impressionistic Horror Night and Campfire Tales Night—during which patrons spontaneously share true tales of paranormal experiences.*

**Right, center:** *Year-round, Harley-Davidson owners gather each week at the Alki Tavern in West Seattle for Taco Thursday. Begun informally ten years ago with a build-your-own, fifty-cent taco night, this ever-popular, sometimes-controversial weekly event has grown into the largest non-sanctioned Harley event in the country, attracting bikers from all over the United States. A record 850 bikers have shown up at the tavern at one time, but usually the numbers are smaller. During the two-to three-hour event, sleek Harley "hogs," some valued at $30,000 or more, are lined up in front of the tavern, across the street, and often spill into surrounding parking lots. Bikers en masse may seem like an intimidating bunch, but it turns out that many are doctors, lawyers, and businessmen who have temporarily shed their professional attire for fringed leather.*

**Right, bottom:** *Serving up memories as much as cheeseburgers, Dick's Drive-In was started in 1954. Not only did most boomers grow up eating the inexpensive quick-fix (Dick's Deluxe, fries, and a shake), but they continue to do so, bringing their kids—and their kids' kids—to the five historic Dick's Drive-In Restaurants located in the Seattle area. If nostalgia could have a taste, this is it.*

Sports are big in Seattle, and here an enthusiastic Seahawks fan shows his team spirit with facepaint and vocals. The Seattle Seahawks are the Northwest's only professional football team and play in the NFL's AFC West Division. Since the Kingdome opened in 1976, the Seahawks have thrilled green-and-blue-bedecked fans at the sixty-six-thousand-seat stadium located just south of Pioneer Square. In 1997, taxpayers voted to build the Seahawks a new home, a state-of-the-art football, soccer, and exhibition stadium which is scheduled to open in 2002.

In 1997, Seattle Mariners' outfielder Ken Griffey Jr. was unanimously voted the American League's Most Valuable Player, becoming just the thirteenth unanimous MVP selection in major league history. Griffey collected an AL-high 56 home runs and 147 runs batted in. In 1997, nearly 3.2 million fans watched the Mariners claim their second division title in three years. The club will begin playing in a new 45,658-seat ballpark, now under construction just south of their present home in the Kingdome, in July 1999. (Photo © Michael Zagaris, Courtesy of the Seattle Mariners)

"Seattle is made up of genuinely nice people who care passionately about their city, the environment, the arts, their sport teams—and support them all."
—Marie Dempcy,
Vice President,
Mayflower Park Hotel

Originally called the Coliseum when it was completed for the 1962 World's Fair, this building subsequently received a $74-million facelift and reopened in the fall of 1995 as the KeyArena. Located on the western edge of the Seattle Center, this is the place to enjoy a full venue of rock concerts, touring ice shows, conventions, and sporting events. KeyArena holds 17,500 cheering fans during home games for the NBA's Seattle SuperSonics. From September to March, screaming, stomping hockey fans fill KeyArena for fast-paced games played by the Seattle Thunderbirds in the Western Hockey League.

Basketball fans love the Seattle SuperSonics and pack KeyArena for their forty-one action-packed home games. The Sonics played in the NBA Finals in 1996, but fell one series short of a championship, losing to Michael Jordan and the Chicago Bulls. Led by all-stars Gary Payton and Vin Baker, and coached by Paul Westphal, the Sonics are now poised to repeat their exciting run to the NBA Finals. (Photo © Jeff Reinking, Courtesy of the Seattle SuperSonics)

Jockeys and their thoroughbred mounts race to the finish line at Emerald Downs in Auburn, south of Seattle. The new 166-acre, world-class horseracing facility opened in 1996 to replace the historic Longacres track, which closed in 1992 after fifty-nine seasons of racing. Emerald Downs offers live racing from March through September, culminating in the $200,000 Longacres Mile. More than five hundred television monitors throughout the stadium keep fans close to the racing action. Beautiful moonrises and an almost touchable Mount Rainier can be enjoyed from the Grandstand.

# Index

# Where to Go for More Information

Seattle-King County Convention and Visitors Bureau. 520 Pike Street, Suite 1300, Seattle, WA 98101. (206) 461-5840. **Information available:** Provides a calendar of events, lodging guide, and visitor guide for the greater Seattle area.

Puget Sound Attractions Council. 217 Ninth Avenue North, Seattle, WA 98109. (206) 623-8632. **Information available:** Offers free *Seattle Favorites* vacation guide featuring twenty-four major attractions within the greater Seattle-Tacoma area.

Washington State Tourism Division. PO Box 42500, Olympia, WA 98504-2500. (800) 544-1800. **Information available:** Distributes a Washington State calendar of events, a getaway guide, and information about travel and lodging.

# About the Author and Photographer

Author Barbara Sleeper moved to Seattle in her youth, and though she has traveled far and wide around the globe, her home has been in or near the city ever since. A freelance writer specializing in travel, wildlife conservation, and science, Barbara is the author of five books in addition to *Seattle* and has published more than three hundred articles in such publications as *Animals, Pacific Discovery, Audubon, Eco Traveler, Life,* and many others.

*Photo © Tom Boyden*

For nearly thirty years, Seattle-based photographer Mike Sedam has specialized in travel photography around the globe. His work has been widely published in the travel industry and in numerous publications. He has published two previous books and is at work on three more. Mike maintains an extensive stock photography library on Seattle and the western United States, including Hawaii.

*Photo © Dan Stearns*